There Were Times I Thought I Was

CRAZY

A Black Woman's Story of Incest

Vanessa Alleyne

Sister Vision
Black Women and Women of Colour Press

96 97 98 99 00 ML 5 4 3 2 1

Canadian Cataloguing in Publication Data

Alleyne, Vanessa
There were times I thought I was CRAZY
ISBN 1-896705-08-1
I. Title
PS8551.L5557T43 1996 C813'-54 C96-932082-5
PR9199.3.A44T43 1996

*The publisher acknowledges the kind assistance of the
Canada Council and the Ontario Arts Council*

Cover painting & design: *Stephanie Martin*
Author photo: *Heather Evans*
Book design and layout: *michèle*

Represented in Canada by the *Literary Press Group*
Distributed in Canada by *General Distribution*
Represented and distributed in the U.S.A. by *LPC Group/InBook*
Represented in Britain by *Turnaround Distribution*

Printed in Canada by union labour

SISTER VISION
Black Women and Women of Colour Press
P.O. Box 217, Station E
Toronto, Ontario
Canada M6H 4E2
(416) 595-5033
e-mail: sisvis@web.net

Dedication

To the memory of my son, Christopher Lee.
To the mother I never had but always loved.
To the nieces and nephews I hope to protect.
And especially to all my sisters who are related to me
through our shared experiences.

I love you all.

Acknowledgements

I would like to thank God for carrying me
at those times in my life when I was too weak to carry myself.
My grandmother, Thelma Alleyne,
for her mothering and for teaching me to trust in God.
The three most important guys in my life — Vinnie, Josh, and Jimmy,
for understanding when I needed my space,
and when I needed the love, hugs and kisses.
My brother, Rodney for continuing to be my brother even through hard times.
The staff at the Oshawa Durham Rape Crisis Centre
for their support, counselling, and court accompaniment.
Sister Vision Press, especially Makeda Silvera: for acknowledging the need to
make stories like mine public, for supporting me and guiding me along this
journey; but mostly, for allowing my voice to be heard.
As this chapter is closed another one begins.

Table of Contents

PUBLISHER'S NOTE 1

PROLOGUE: *My Mother* 3

PART I 11

PART II 111

EPILOGUE 163

Publisher's Note

This is not a work of fiction. It is a true account of the physical, sexual and psychological abuse that Vanessa Alleyne suffered at the hands of her stepfather, of the aftermath of that abuse and of her attempts to bring him to justice. In the Prologue, Vanessa draws on the recollections of family and friends to piece together the events leading up to her birth. The chapters which follow trace her courageous journey to unearth the secrets of her past, to restore her belief in her memory and in her sanity. Throughout the book, pseudonyms have been adopted, but the incidents described did happen, and the people are real. Her family's refusal to acknowledge what happened, combined with the inadequacy or incompetence of the institutions that were supposed to protect and defend her, has meant that Vanessa has not seen justice done. Many people have taken her stepfather's word over hers. Others have believed and supported Vanessa. We think you will too.

PROLOGUE

My Mother

June Alleyne spent most of her youth dreaming of getting off the small island of Trinidad and going to the big exciting world of North America. She wasn't one to listen to the advice of her five older sisters, nor anyone else, for that matter. As a teenager, she learned how to sneak in and out of her bedroom window at night without getting caught. Stealth was necessary, because her father and mother wouldn't have thought twice about giving her a good licking for leaving the house so late. Luckily for June, her younger brother was very fond of his outgoing sister, and willingly helped her.

Of her older sisters, June was closest to the outspoken Daisy, who had a reputation as a "hot girl." By the time June was seventeen, she and Daisy were regulars at the local night spots. Not surprisingly, when Daisy fell in love with a handsome young Indian man named Peter Turnbull, June started seeing Peter's identical twin, Paul.

"I cyah believe dis," June cried. But she finally had to admit to herself that she was pregnant.

June's parents had no idea that she was having sex. She knew if they found out she'd probably receive a memorable whipping from them both.

The first person June revealed her pregnancy to was her sister and best friend. Daisy's shock was overshadowed by her envy. She herself had been pregnant by Peter, but it had been a tubal pregnancy, and had ended with an operation. Many tears had been shed.

June desperately wanted an abortion, but she couldn't bring herself to tell Daisy, for fear of hurting her. Daisy pleaded with her to have the baby, and to give it to her to raise.

"I cyah give you mih baby," June protested.

"But yuh thinking about throwing it away, not so?"

"Is up to me what I go do. I go make up mih own mind."

One evening, June went to the home of a medicine woman.

"Yuh mudder know yuh here?" the woman asked her.

"Yes. Is she who tell me where to go."

The old woman looked June over, then went up to her and placed her hands on June's belly.

"Well," she said, looking up, "Yuh makin chile, ah sure ah dat."

"Yuh could help mih?"

"I could give yuh sometin', but if it wock or not is up to the good Lord. I eh have no control over who born in dis world or who eh born, yuh hear."

"I cyah have dis chile." June was close to tears. "It go mess up mih whole life."

"Huh! Well look at my crosses! It sound to me like you shoulda think about dat long before yuh gone and open up yuh legs. Is your own problem getting in all dis trouble. I know all yuh mammy bring all yuh up better than dat. Jes because yuh big sister an dem gone an have chile, it don't mean you have to follow dem. Buh look at you, now yuh doin de same ting." She went into another room in the small house.

June sat down and inwardly cursed the woman for trying to make her feel guilty.

"How come she eh do it for you sheself?"

"What?" said June, confused.

"Yuh mammy. She coulda do it for you sheself. She know jes as much as me, if not more."

June bowed her head, wishing she could just get it over with without having to answer all these questions.

"Here," the woman said, handing June a small bottle containing a green liquid. "Yuh drink all ah dis, and make sure yuh have a latrine near — yuh go need it." With that, she disappeared into the other room.

June pretended to be bedridden for a day, then she drank the potion. The bleeding started almost immediately.

On the second day, June awoke to find herself soaked with blood. The blood had also soiled the two sisters who shared her bed.

"Yuh awright?" asked one.

"Yes, I awright," said June. "Is jes dat ah find ah lil' heavy dis month, dat is all."

"Yuh should take a purge," offered the other sister.

"I eh need no purge. Look, jes leave me alone, yuh hear," June replied curtly, and began changing the bedclothes.

For many days the blood flowed; June was relieved to see that it was so easy. Her stomach cramped constantly, and she broke into cold sweats.

The rest of the household paid very little attention to her condition. Those who noticed minded their own business.

A few weeks later, June was dismayed to realize that her period was late. She waited for another month. No period. Her breasts were starting to feel tender, and her pants felt snug.

"When yuh going to tell mammy yuh pregnant?" Daisy asked one day.

"I take some medicine and I eh pregnant again."

"What yuh mean you take medicine? What medicine yuh take? When?"

"I get it from dat crazy woman up the hill. Was some weeks ago."

"Yuh must be blasted crazy! Dat woman is a witch! What de hell yuh tink yuh was doing to go to she?"

"Is my body and is my damn business!"

A few days later, June had just taken a bath and was preparing to get dressed, when her mother came into her room.

"Doh put nutten on yet," she ordered June. "Come here."

June did as she was told. Her mother started to feel her belly.

"Who you was with?" her mother asked.

"Nobody."

"Yuh tink I blind?" Her mother slapped her across the face. "Yuh standin up here in front of mih pregnant and still yuh saying yuh didn't take no man?"

"Mammy, I not pregnant."

Her mother slapped her again. "Put on yuh clothes. And doh leave dis room, yuh hear. What yuh think yuh father going to do when he find out dat yuh have a belly? Yuh always with some boy, and now yuh gone and get yuhself in trouble."

June sat on the bed and started to cry. She'd suspected that the medicine hadn't worked but had refused to believe it. She had noticed the changes in her body, but had been hoping they didn't mean anything.

"Yuh more than four months," said her mother before leaving. "How long yuh tink dis go be a secret?"

Her parents punished June by beating her regularly. Between beatings, her mother demanded that June tell her who the father was.

"I doh know his name," June insisted. She and Daisy were no longer seeing the brothers. After Peter had beaten her senseless, Daisy had gone to live with an aunt on the other side of the island. June wanted nothing more to do with Peter or Paul.

"How yuh could be pregnant for somebody and doh know what he name?"

"But mammy, it was only one time."

"Yuh think all ah we stupid or what?"

"Ah telling de truth. He say he from de University. Daisy and me went to look for him there, but we couldn't find him at all."

"You jes keep yuhself in the house and let me deal with Daisy." But Daisy, when asked, had nothing to add about the baby's father.

No one in the family ever mentioned June's pregnancy openly. There were a lot of whispers, with everyone trying to guess who the man was. She lived out the last few months of her pregnancy in quiet disgrace, hardly ever going out and rarely seeing her few friends.

When she went into labour, her father refused to assist or even acknowledge it, though he worked as a nurse and could easily have helped. June was taken to the hospital by her mother. Mrs. Alleyne loved June, as she did all her kids, but she also believed June had done wrong. Besides, she had learned the hard way not to cross her husband — it was common practice for men to beat their women into submission.

It was a long and hard labour. June gave birth to a healthy baby girl on February 13, 1968. The pain left her exhausted and angry, but she also felt a bit amused at the sight of the baby's few strands of straight black hair. Her mother also liked looking at the little half-Indian baby.

Daisy started visiting June's baby regularly. She liked to pretend that the pretty little girl was her own. One day, in June's absence, she took the child to visit some friends.

"Look yuh daughter, Paul. She name Sharon Ann Vanessa."

"Yuh mean Baldy," Peter answered for his brother. "She eh have no hair."

Paul held the baby in his arms for a brief moment. Whatever he felt could not be seen in his eyes.

Daisy moved back into her parents' house temporarily, and between her, her sisters and their mother, the baby was looked after. Always in the care of her family, little Sharon was the "pet" everyone loved to play with, and so she came to be known as Pet. Her hair started to grow, and she ran around with little curls hanging in her face.

Just after Pet's first birthday, Daisy offered to buy her. June had the adoption papers drawn up, but at the last minute her mother and other sisters talked her out of selling her baby. Daisy was very hurt by this, but June agreed to let Pet live with Daisy and her new fiance.

Meanwhile, June met and fell in love with a man named Tony. She was thrilled to find out that he had family in North America and planned to move there. She ignored the whispers about Tony.

"Dat man is a no good, June. He on drugs, and he have girls up an down in de street," her friends told her.

"All ah dat is jes ole talk. Allyuh jes jealous, all ah allyuh jealous."

She was in love, so she was not too upset when she found out she was pregnant again. After all, she thought, he loves me. He's going to take me to Canada and take care of me.

She gave birth to a baby boy. This time, her mother delivered the baby herself, at home in a back room.

"Keep de baby quiet," said Mrs. Alleyne.

The baby was named Jerome John.

When Jerome was just a few weeks old, Pet moved back in with her grandmother and aunts. Daisy and her fiance were going to America, and June was going to Canada with Jerome's father. Daisy hated to leave the child, whom she now thought of as her own and who called her Mommy.

June and Tony moved to Canada, and June became a Canadian citizen. The couple then moved to New York City for a few years. June gave birth to Pet's two youngest brothers, Leonard and Simon. There were rumours that Tony was violent. Eventually she divorced him. Shortly afterwards, she married a man named Ralph Godfrey. She returned to Canada alone. Due to various problems with Immigration, Ralph remained in their New York apartment with the two little boys. June applied for permits to bring Pet and Jerome to Canada.

More than ten years after leaving for North America, June returned to Trinidad to fetch her children. But once there, she didn't have enough money to bring both children back to Canada. She decided to bring only the younger one.

"You not going to carry Jerome and leave Pet behind, yuh hear?" her mother scolded her. "You done leave de two a dem here long enough. Pet getting to be a young lady now and she need she mother."

"But I doh have enough money for de plane tickets."

"Jes leh me worry about dat. Listen, yuh have to promise me you go look out for Pet. She kinda delicate and she is a smart child. Don't keep she wocking all the time yuh hear, take some time to get to know de girl."

As soon as she was alone, Mrs. Alleyne emptied the pan where she hid her savings, and counted out the exact amount for Pet's plane ticket, some of it in quarters and pennies.

On September 8, 1980, June and her two children left Trinidad on a BWIA flight.

"Pet," she said to her daughter as they sat together on the plane, "yuh nearly twelve years now. Yuh have to use yuh real name from now on. If anybody ask yuh, tell them yuh name is Vanessa."

Part I

CHAPTER ONE

The Pre-Trial: 1993

I sat in the almost-empty Toronto courtroom and looked across at my stepfather. He sat alone as his lawyer and the Crown attorney discussed something with the judge. The only other people at the hearing were my counsellors, Susie and Maia from the Oshawa Durham Rape Crisis Centre. Detective Murray was there, as promised, and a man sat alone in the very back row.

On the first day of the preliminary hearing, my mother had been asked to leave the courtroom because she might be called by Ralph's lawyer, or even by mine, as a hostile witness. Today she remained out in the corridor, and I hadn't had a chance to see her eyes. The first day, before she'd gone out, I had seen her anger at me in her eyes, but she also looked as though she was about to cry.

Susie had given me one of her earrings to hold onto in the witness box. I used it as a crutch, turning it around and around in my hands as Ralph's lawyer asked me the same questions over and over. He had also represented my stepfather back in 1983, the first time he was charged. I'd never met him before, but judging from his attitude, I hadn't missed much.

"When your father raped you, Vanessa, you claim that you were home alone. Why?"

I pricked my finger with Susie's earring to remind myself to keep my cool and not yell at him. He had been questioning me for the past hour. Often he would seem to forget that I had just answered one of his questions. He would look at his copy of my statement and ask the same question two minutes later. I looked around at Detective Murray, the judge, Susie and Maia; every one of them looked frustrated.

Finally, the judge told the lawyer, "Move along. I don't have all day."

My only regret as I answered the questions was that my mother wasn't in the courtroom to hear me. I wanted so much for her to finally listen to me without changing the subject. I'd started this trial mainly so that she and Ralph would be forced to listen to me.

Every now and then Ralph would look at me and frown, as if to warn me. I stared at him the whole time I was being questioned; my eyes only left him to glance at my counsellors for support or to look at the lawyer and the judge. I wanted to make sure he heard everything I said. No running away — no place to hide.

The Crown attorney had explained to me that there was a chance that the charges would be thrown out of court, because my stepfather had already faced those charges ten years earlier, in 1983. Something about his rights. I couldn't see why he had so many rights.

The good thing was that if we did get to trial, we stood a pretty good chance of getting a conviction. Why Ralph wanted a jury trial, I don't know. I just wanted it over and done with.

Just when I was beginning to wonder how much longer I could hold myself together, his lawyer said, "No more questions."

I looked over at Susie and saw the relief on her face. We both knew that if we succeeded in taking the case to trial and getting a conviction, we'd be setting a strong legal precedent for women who had been assaulted, raped, and abused, and for the agencies that support these women. Women all over Canada could feel less afraid to come forward, even after years of silence and secret pain.

"You may step down."

I made my way over to Susie and Maia. As I passed by, Detective Murray gave me a wink, as if to say "Good job."

"What do you think?" I whispered to Susie in the silence that followed.

"The judge will give his decision soon."

I turned to Maia. "How did I do?"

"You were great!"

Sitting between the two counsellors, I allowed myself to relax and closed my eyes for a minute, trying to silence the questions in my head. The lawyer had asked so many questions, demanded so much detail. I wished I could have left all those memories shut up in my mind. Saying them out loud felt dirty. To comfort me, Susie held one of my hands, and Maia held the other. I forced myself to look composed so that my stepfather couldn't see how worried I was.

I had been really upset, years ago, when the charges against Ralph were dropped while I was in the group home. Now I realized that back then, in the midst of my breakdown, I would never have been able to control my emotions. Being in court now, having had ten years to mature and develop my own sense of worth, was the best thing. Though nothing could have prepared me for the feelings that flooded me as soon as the questioning began, I'd known what I would be in for, and having the support of the rape crisis centres and other women's agencies helped give me the strength to proceed.

I wondered what my mother was doing, out in the corridor. Was she pacing the floor or wringing her hands? Was she worried about the judge's ruling? I still knew so little about her.

In all the time I lived with June and Ralph, I never once saw them kiss or hold hands. I never even saw them sit next to each other, except in the car. Now, I had finally seen her hold his hand. They had been holding onto each other during the last session. Whether they were really comforting each other, or whether it was all for show, I wasn't sure. Their eyes told no stories. Their faces showed nothing.

Susie nudged me. Ralph and his lawyer were standing. We didn't have long to wait.

"I find that there is enough evidence to proceed to trial..."

The judge was saying something else, but his words sounded distant. All I heard were those first words: *Enough evidence to proceed to trial.*

I was quickly ushered out of the courtroom by Susie and Maia. Maia walked on with me, while Susie went back to speak to Detective Murray.

"So what does it all mean?" I asked Maia.

"It means that you're going to trial, silly." She smiled.

Susie, Maia and I went down to the cafeteria to avoid bumping into my mother and stepfather. In silence, we each lit up a cigarette.

"Well, so far so good," Susie said finally.

"You were excellent," Maia told me.

"The only thing you did wrong was that you gave out too much information," said Susie. "When we go to trial, just answer his lawyer's questions. If he doesn't have all the facts, that's his problem."

"Well, he was getting all the information mixed up. I was just correcting him. Anyway, I don't have anything to hide or to be ashamed of."

"Yeah, but don't help him by giving him information he should already have if he read your transcript properly. That's his job — let him do it. But don't worry — you're doing just great."

Half an hour later, June, Ralph and his lawyer walked by us. We turned and looked at them. My mother and my stepfather made no attempt to be close; the lawyer walked between them. Strange, I thought. I inhaled the smoke from my cigarette and watched in silence, wondering what they were thinking.

The drive home was mostly quiet, with occasional snippets of conversation. When we got to my house, I thanked Susie and Maia for being there for me.

"I'll call you if I hear anything from Detective Murray or the Crown," Susie promised.

"You stay strong and try not to think about it too much. You've got a good bit of time before the trial begins," said Maia, squeezing my hand.

"I'll keep in touch," I promised, and went inside.

Alone in my living room, I chain-smoked, and opened a bottle of wine. Nursing a glass, I went over the events of the past year. So much information in such a short time. Who would have thought that after all this time, justice was coming my way?

I finished the glass of wine, left the house and got into my car. There was somewhere I had to go right away. There was someone who had to be told what had happened.

As I turned into the driveway, I could almost hear my heart beating. I was excited, but I wasn't frightened any more. I pulled over to Section Eleven and got out of the car, taking the flowers I'd picked up on the way over. I lit another cigarette, walked over to the spot and laid the flowers on the grave.

I stood looking at the flowers in silence. It had been hard to get forget-me-nots — I'd called three florists before I found some. They looked nice on the grave. The card read: "Just like I promised. Love, Mommy."

I ground out the cigarette and knelt down by the grave. I thought back to what had happened in court that day. I remembered Ralph's face when the judge gave his decision. He looked shocked, as if he hadn't thought it possible to be forced to go to trial after all that time. In all the time I'd known him, I'd never seen him look defeated.

"Everything is going to fall into place," I whispered. "What goes around comes around, Christopher Lee. Soon you'll be able to rest in peace, and so will I."

I wiped away my tears and got up to leave.

"I'll be back when it's over. I'll bring you all the good news."

I kissed the card that I'd stapled to the flowers and left the cemetery where my son was buried. I would not return till the trial was over.

CHAPTER TWO

1983

It was cold that night in January. I remember going into my brother Jerome's room. He was the oldest of my three younger brothers and the one I felt closest to. We'd shared a bedroom back in Trinidad, with him on the bottom bunk and me on the top. The pain was back again. I lay down beside Jerome and started to cry.

"Is it still hurting?"

"Yes," I replied, in a voice that sounded strange to me. "It won't stop."

We lay on his bed, without speaking, waiting for the pain to go away. I was fourteen and Jerome was thirteen.

I hugged my chest and started to rock back and forth. I cried and prayed to God to take the pain away. Then I slid off the bed as quietly as I had got on. I could see tears in Jerome's eyes as I left. I wanted to tell him that things were going to be all right, but I felt faint and it was all I could do to make my way to the bathroom. I leaned up against the wall in the hallway, wanting to vomit. I took a few deep breaths, holding each one before letting it go, then continued towards the bathroom. I was dizzy and I felt my stomach muscles tightening. Before I could grab hold of something for support, I passed out.

When I came to, I found myself on the bathroom floor. I pulled myself up and sat on the toilet. I could feel a tingling, a feeling of something dripping between my legs. My first thought when I saw that my nightclothes were soaked was that I had wet myself. I sat on the toilet and waited for the fluid to stop, but it kept flowing, ever so slowly.

I still couldn't understand why this was happening to me. I felt embarrassed. I had lost control of everything, including my bodily functions, and I had not slept in almost three days. I fought back sleep, but I could not fight back the tears. Something was desperately wrong with me, and I would have to ask my mother for help.

For months I had spoken to my mother only when she spoke to me, which was not often. It had been this way since my pregnancy was confirmed. I had made a vow not to ask her for anything, but now I had no choice. More than the physical pain, knowing that I had lost another battle was making me cry. He'd won again. They always won.

It was getting hard for me to breathe. I could feel another dizzy spell coming on. I tried to brace myself for it. Getting back onto the toilet, I tried to fight the urge to push long and hard. The pain intensified.

I made my way back to my brother's room. He was wide awake, sitting up in bed. Crying, I sat down beside him. He looked worried.

Jerome looked a lot older than his years. Even when we were in Trinidad, he'd looked like that.

Often, we had wondered about our mother.

"What yuh tink she looking like now?" he would ask me.

"I ain't *think*. I *know* my mother is de most beautiful woman in America."

One day, Jerome and I were walking down the big hill near Grams's house, taking the garbage out for pick-up. The pick-up site was a little way from our house and it was our job to sweep the yard every day and carry out the garbage. I had the biggest buckets, and Jerome had two smaller ones — one balanced on his head, the other held in his hand. When we were halfway down the hill, we saw a plane zooming across the sky.

"What if she comin' in that plane?" Jerome asked.

"She going to bring plenty toys and ting for we."

"Maybe she comin' to get we to come and live with she."

We sat down on the hill, and watched the plane go by.

"What yuh tink she leave we for?" Jerome asked.

"I tink is because we older and smarter than we brothers."

There was one time when Jerome and I really missed having a mother around. It happened one day when I was around ten. Our grandfather had accused us of stealing twenty cents. I knew we hadn't stolen the money, and so did Jerome, but our grandfather insisted on punishing us both. He beat us with a tree branch until he saw that we were both blistered. Then he had us kneel on the concrete with big stones in our hands. Under the hot sun, with no protection for our knees, it wasn't long before the weight of the stones began to bend our elbows.

"Doh move," Grandfather snapped, hitting me with the tree branch. "Stay right dey till I hear yuh say yuh take de money."

"I eh sayin nutten," I cried, but before I could say any more he slapped my face so hard I saw stars.

I looked at my cousins standing around and laughing, and I wanted to get up and punch each one in the stomach. I hated to see my brother kneeling and crying.

"If ah say dat ah take de money, we could get up?" I asked.

He nodded. I put my pride and innocence on hold.

"Awright, I take de money and everything else. I do everything." I waited. "Now we could get up?"

Our grandfather walked over to Jerome, took the stones from his hands and let him get up. I smiled at my brother, hoping he could see how smart I was. With no father, and a mother in America, I knew I had to look out for Jerome and myself.

"You stay right here," Grandfather said to me. He left me kneeling in the sun.

I prayed silently that my mother would hurry up and get us out of that house. I wondered whether the others would have been nicer to us if she was still with us.

Soon afterwards, Jerome got sick and had to be taken to the hospital. It turned out that he had worms in his head, from carrying buckets of garbage balanced on his head. The dirty water had been seeping through his hair. He was away from home for over a week.

Jerome still had a nearly-bald patch on his head from his bout with the worms, and he hoped that one day his hair would grow back. As I looked into his eyes, I wished again that our mother would come and save us. The difference was that now our mother was in the next room.

We got dressed and snuck downstairs and out of the house. The fresh air felt good on my face. We had moved here four months earlier. We were in an Ontario Housing Complex, where most of the tenants were single-parent families, or on welfare or with low incomes. We were a low-income family; my stepfather didn't work. This house was a lot bigger than our last one, and it had been exciting for me to have my own bedroom at last.

Jerome and I walked across the street to the park.

"We could run away," he said. "Nobody would know who we were. We could change our names."

"I'm not running anywhere. I'm not the one who should be running away."

My pajama bottoms were soaked. The pain, which had started two days ago, got worse. I clenched my teeth and started to moan again.

"I'm going to die."

Jerome looked bewildered but didn't say anything.

"You know, I never thought that dying was going to hurt so much. As a matter of fact, I didn't think this much pain was possible. But in a way I'm glad it's happening. I won't have to deal with them any more. I just hope that it happens fast."

I was running out of time. I wanted to tell my brother everything I needed him to do for me after I was dead.

"Tell Grams that I love her and I'll miss her. And don't forget to tell everyone that it wasn't my fault."

"You can't miss someone when you're dead," Jerome objected. I could see that he was just as frightened as I was.

He said, "Let's just go inside and tell her that you're not feeling well."

We got up and started back towards the house. I prayed that my mother wouldn't laugh at me and that I wouldn't have to speak to my stepfather ever again. I prayed that I would die. I started to hum an old song that Grams used to sing to me at night when I was afraid. It didn't make me feel any better. But I decided I was not going to be afraid. I straightened my back and walked tall into the house, ready to face my mother for the last time.

"You'd better go back to your room so you don't get into trouble," I told Jerome. It was after three in the morning, and he was supposed to be asleep.

I took a few more quick breaths and knocked on my parents' bedroom door. No answer. I waited a little while before knocking again, a bit louder. The pain just seemed to be getting worse, but I hesitated before knocking a third time. I was about to go back to my room when I heard movement on the other side of the door.

"Who's there?" Ralph asked. From his tone it was clear he wasn't happy to be awakened.

"It's Pet. I need to speak to my mother."

"Do you know what time it is?"

"Yes. I need to speak to her *now*."

As I stood listening to him trying to wake my mother, I tried to think of something nice about Ralph. I knew almost nothing about him. He was born in Barbados. He had a son somewhere. I knew that he met my mother when she was living in Brooklyn, that she married him a few years ago and that he had lived with her and my two younger brothers before Jerome and I came to stay with them. But that was all. I wondered if he had always been the way he was now, or if he had gotten this way as he got older.

June came out of the bedroom, half asleep. "What is it?"

"I'm sick. I've been trying to use the bathroom all night. My whole body is hurting and I can't stop peeing."

She grew more alert.

"I think I'm constipated," I said. I felt foolish having to explain such personal details to her.

She placed her hand on my belly. As she felt around, I thought I saw a slight smile on her face. She seemed to understand my situation. I had feared that she would be harsh with me, especially since she had ordered me to stay locked in my room after the last run-in with Ralph.

Three days earlier, I had stayed home from school because I wasn't feeling well. Ralph took the phone off the hook so I couldn't dial out.

"Why do you keep taking the phone off the hook?"

Without a word, he walked past me and out of the house, leaving the phone in his room off the hook, and the door to his room locked. When he came back two hours later, I was furious.

"I was supposed to call my teacher so she could bring by some homework for me."

"That's your problem."

"Why do you keep doing all this stupid stuff?"

"Why do you have to be such a little bitch all the time?"

He stood in the kitchen pouring himself some juice, looking at me in amusement. He was shorter than my mother and very dark. He was slim and had a smaller frame than my mother's ex-husband. He wore his hair in a short afro and had a small beard.

I knew that he didn't love my mother — he had told me so, many times. But I couldn't understand why he enjoyed hurting me.

To my surprise, when my mother came home that evening, she punished me for swearing at Ralph and for threatening to break up their relationship.

"That's not true!" I screamed. "Why do you always listen to everything he tells you? Why don't you believe it when I tell you he raped me and he still wants to have sex with me whenever you're not here?"

"Get upstairs to your room and close the door. And don't come out until I say you can!"

I went upstairs, kind of happy to be locked away from everyone. Then the pain started.

"Go and get dressed," my mother told me. "We're going to the hospital."

I went back to my room and leaned on the wall to catch my breath. I could hear her explaining to Ralph that she needed to take me to the hospital. He said something — I couldn't hear what, but I could tell that they were disagreeing.

Jerome came into my room, looking puzzled.

"You're going to the hospital. I heard ... I guess I'll see you when you come back. Good luck."

He went out again. I could hear him settling himself back into his bed.

I put my ear back to the wall. My parents were still talking. I couldn't believe what I heard.

"You *know* she put that Bible under our bed, so I wouldn't be able to get an erection for you. It wasn't my fault last night," Ralph was saying. "Your mother taught her witchcraft. She's trying to turn you against me. This is all just part of her plan ... She won't stop until she breaks us up. She doesn't want us to be together, June ... You don't really think that I would have sex with her when I'm perfectly happy with you, do you? None of your family likes me and you know it. Your mother put her up to this."

How could she let him talk about Grams like that? I turned away from the wall and started to get dressed. As I was lifting a sweater over my head, I noticed for the first time just how big the bulge in my belly was. Before, when I was changing or taking a bath, I would always close my eyes, never looking at my body until I was fully dressed. I couldn't face the fact that there was a baby inside of me, let alone that it was my stepfather's. When I thought about it, I felt embarrassed and dirty. I was only fourteen, and I knew that my situation was not normal. I told only those people who were very close to me.

My mother came into my room as soon as I was dressed. I wondered if she would miss me in a little while, when I was dead. Looking at her, I felt helpless. She always seemed in control; she never allowed herself to ask for help. I remembered a day, two years earlier, when she, Jerome and I were visiting Jerome's father, her ex-husband. We had been staying at his place for less than a week when he told her to leave. She didn't have to be told twice. She packed our things and we spent that night in a park. I remembered how proud I felt that night.

"The cab is here," said my mother. "Hurry up. The meter's running." She turned and went out. I followed her downstairs and out to the cab. By the time I got outside she was already speaking to the driver, instructing him to take me to the emergency room at the hospital.

Getting into the cab, I saw that June had put a towel on the seat, so I wouldn't soil it. She helped me to get comfortable and then, to my surprise, she got in with me.

"Are you all right?" she asked.

I couldn't bring myself to answer, so I just nodded. I wanted her to go on — I wanted to hear her say that things would be all right from now on, that we could start to work on being a family. But she didn't.

CHAPTER THREE

The ride to the hospital was short and quiet. The pains in my belly were becoming more frequent and lasting longer.

The cab driver pulled up in front of the emergency room. June paid him and we went in. She went to speak to the receptionist, while I sat in one of the few empty chairs. June came over to me with some forms, which she told me to sign. I did, then she took them and filled in the blanks. There were questions about my family doctor's name and address, about my blood type, about the baby's father and about my health number.

A few minutes later, a heavy-set nurse took the completed forms from June. She looked them over, and I could see that she was surprised by what she read. She asked June some questions about my pains and how long I'd been in labour. I couldn't understand why she didn't ask me — I was sitting right there. She told June that there were some tests they needed to do. I got up and followed the nurse.

She took me to a room, and told me to undress. She gave me a plain white hospital gown, one of the kind that don't close in the back.

"You'll be taken upstairs for an ultrasound. The doctor will be looking at you shortly." She didn't make a big deal out of it. She left, and I was in the room by myself.

Two men dressed in blue came into the room with a wheelchair.

"Ready to go?" asked one of them.

I nodded, and watched as they prepared the chair. They put me in it, wheeled me upstairs and left me in another room. I wondered what they all thought of me — a pregnant fourteen-year-old.

A young nurse came in and wheeled me into yet another room. She asked in a friendly voice, "Can you stand?"

"Yes."

"All right then. Why don't you help me get you up onto this table?"

Lifting up the gown, she rubbed a kind of jelly on my abdomen. She placed a cold metal instrument on it, and started making circular motions with it. As she worked, she kept her eyes on the monitor in front of her.

In the same friendly tone, she asked, "So what's your name?"

"Vanessa. But my family call me Pet."

"Pet. That's a cute name."

I realized she was not really listening to me. All her attention was focused on the screen. She paused every now and then to smile and nod at me. After a few minutes of this, she left the room, then returned with a man shorter than herself.

"Hi Vanessa," he said. "My name is Dr. Albert. Let's see what the problem is here." He started to move the instrument on my belly, as the nurse had done before. He explained the signs of labour to me and asked me how long I'd been feeling pains. When we figured out that I'd been in labour for almost thirty-six hours, he looked troubled.

"Why did it take you so long to come to the hospital?"

I kept quiet. How could I tell him that when I went into labour, I thought God was finally answering my prayers and preparing to take my life? I felt foolish.

"Get her ready for surgery," he ordered the nurse.

Confused, I started to cry again.

In yet another room, two new nurses shaved my genital area and abdomen. I watched them in despair. Dr. Albert came in, and lifted my legs onto two metal bars at the end of the bed. He then put on a white latex glove and pushed his hand into my vagina. It felt as though I was being ripped in half.

"There's a bit of a problem. You have a breech delivery on your hands. The baby hasn't turned, and there's really no option but to take it out by C-section."

He removed his hand and left. I felt even more confused. Maybe it was all a dream.

The heavy-set nurse walked in with more forms for me to sign. Everyone seemed to be paying a lot more attention to me now; they moved around hurriedly. Three more nurses came in and started to get the equipment ready.

"Turn on your side and bring your knees up towards your chest," one told me. Before I could protest, one nurse was holding me down, while another roughly pulled my knees to my chest and lifted my gown. The third nurse came towards me holding a large needle. She leaned over and stuck it into my back. The sharp prick startled me. Then it was over and they let go of me. I felt bruised from their rough handling.

They went over to a table at the other end of the room, where one of them filled out a form while the other two looked over at me.

"Did you know she's only fourteen?"

"They just seem to be getting younger and younger every day."

"You'd think that if they're old enough to open their legs, they'd be old enough to stand the pain," said the first nurse.

"Is the baby's father with her?" the third nurse asked.

"No," said the first. "I'd be surprised if she even knows who he is. Her mother's here, poor woman. Not even *she* knows who the father is. The girl won't tell her anything."

"The poor lady," said the second nurse. "Can you imagine what she must be going through? A daughter in this condition at such a young age."

"You know girls," said the third nurse, shaking her head. "They stray, but they always come home crying." She turned to look at me. "Look at her. Her mother is having an awful time, and all she can do is cry."

I wanted to scream at them. How could they believe I'd brought this on myself? I wanted to make them listen to me. But I could only lie there and cry. Eventually, they ended their chatter and took me to an operating room. I tried to move but couldn't move my legs — not even my toes. It felt as if I was strapped to the bed. I was exhausted, and I didn't understand what was happening. In desperation and disgust, I allowed my eyes to close.

CHAPTER FOUR

I saw Ralph coming towards me again. His face looked blurry, but I could see that he was smiling. He was towering over me. Therewas no point in trying to fight him. He always won. June believed everything he told her. I was exhausted, tired of fighting with everyone, tired of trying to make people believe me. All I wanted was for June to make him stop hurting me.

He moved closer, and I held my breath. But just as I was about to shout, "Leave me alone!" I saw his face clearly.

It was Dr. Albert.

Awake now, I listened as he explained to me the procedure I was about to undergo. It would take awhile, he said, but I'd have lots of time to rest up afterwards.

"You'll be a mother in a little while," he said, and left.

The next thing I recall is a brightly-lit room, and a green hospital blanket concealing the lower half of my body. I was surprised to see June sitting on a chair next to my head. When she saw my eyes were open, she said, "This is it. They're going to take the baby out."

It was the first time I had heard her acknowledge that there was a baby inside me.

"Are you all right?" she asked.

I was crying. "I don't know. I'm scared."

"Well, this is no time to be afraid. You have to start thinking about the baby."

What was going on in her mind? Why was she being nice to me all of a sudden? But though I questioned her motives, I wanted more than anything to believe she did care about what was happening to me.

I was slipping in and out of consciousness when the doctor came into the operating room. June watched him, listening to what he was saying to the nurses. I suddenly realized that for some time she had been holding my hand. I wanted to stay awake and see what was going to happen. Everyone around me seemed to be moving in slow motion, preparing for some ritual. I heard bits of conversation but was unable to make any sense of it. I couldn't see the lower half of my body because of the green blanket, and the oxygen mask over my face was making me feel dizzy. All the bright lights in the room were turned directly at me.

There was a lot of pulling and tugging. The pain I'd felt earlier had gone. I heard them cutting something; the sound seemed to echo in my ears. Tears were forming in June's eyes. The doctor spoke to a nurse, then he was pulling something from inside me. There was silence.

One of the nurses turned to my mother.

"It's a boy."

Tears flowed down June's cheeks as she watched the nurse clean the baby. I had never seen her cry before. Was it for the baby, for me or for herself? She continued to hold my hand.

The doctors and nurses were still working on my body. I felt faint. As my eyes closed, I could hear the doctor saying something to me about the baby. The only part I understood was, "It's almost over."

I dozed off for what seemed like a few minutes. It was only when I came to that I realized, in horror, that the cutting the doctor and nurses had been doing earlier was actually on me. They had taken the baby from inside me — the baby boy the nurses were now looking after. I hadn't even realized that the operation had started. I felt used, and more mixed up than ever.

I heard it cry. It wasn't like a real cry — more like a wind-up doll making mechanical noises. June had gone to stand beside the nurse who was caring for the baby. The nurse said something to her, then handed over the small bundle, wrapped in white blankets. They went out of the room.

I woke up alone again, in yet another strange room. I saw a young nurse pass by, but when I tried to call out to her, I gagged. They had put a hose in my throat. When the nurse came over and took out the hose, I almost threw up. She took my temperature, then left without a word.

After I'd been lying there for a while, feeling helpless, the nurse came back.

"Have you regained any feeling in your legs?"

I hadn't. They felt as if they were cast in cement.

Two workers transferred me to another bed and took me back to the maternity ward. My eyes lingered on the nursery as we passed it. I wondered if the baby was in there. The workers took me to a room where two new mothers were feeding their babies. One of the workers pulled a curtain around my bed.

I was starting to feel a tingling in my legs. A nurse came in, took a urine bag from under the bed and emptied it. I didn't know where the urine was coming from. Seeing the look on my face, she explained, "You'll be using this bag until you feel well enough to walk to the bathroom."

Judging from the way I felt just then, it seemed obvious to me that I'd be using these bags for the rest of my life.

I woke up later to find June sitting by my bed. She started talking when she saw that I was awake. It took me a few seconds to understand she was talking about the baby.

"You're going to have to give him a name, you know."

"How am I supposed to do that?"

"This is no time to start acting like a child, Pet. You're a mother now, and you'd better start acting like one."

"How am I supposed to name a baby?"

I was still very disoriented, and I didn't feel like talking about the baby. I wanted the baby to go away and leave me alone. I wished the baby had never happened.

"He's very small — only four pounds, nine ounces," she said, then added casually, "You'd better name him soon. It doesn't look like he's going to make it."

"What do you mean, he's not going to make it?"

A feeling of loss came over me, which was strange as this was possibly the best news I'd heard in years. Why was I feeling this way?

"He's very premature, and his lungs are underdeveloped. He's being monitored."

"Is he going to die?"

"Yes." There was no emotion in her voice.

I was silent for a while, trying to digest this. Then out of the blue I said, "Christopher Lee, I guess."

"I have to go," she replied. "I'll be back soon."

I felt glad that she'd asked me to name the baby, though I didn't understand why. Suddenly I had been given a say in things.

When one of the babies in the room started to cry, I felt guilty, as if I was responsible for the problems my own baby was having. I wondered if babies understood each other. Maybe this crying baby was bringing me a message from my own child. I tried to picture my own baby. I had the urge to tell him I was sorry.

Two nurses came to get me out of bed and into a wheelchair. One told me, "You may see your baby now. He's in an incubator and is quite small. Don't be alarmed by his size."

My whole body ached. I still couldn't move my legs on my own. If I'd had the strength to speak, I would have said that I didn't want to see the baby. I pictured tiny little horns growing from the top of his head, and webs between his fingers and toes. I imagined bright fire-red eyes. I was afraid to be in the same room with him.

I tried to be strong as one of the nurses wheeled me into the dark room. She pushed me up to a small glass case and said, "I'll be back for you in a few minutes."

I sat in the wheelchair with my eyes closed for a few minutes, trying to gather the courage to turn around and look into the glass case. The hustle and bustle of the hospital seemed miles away, and the dim lighting in the room added to my unease. Finally, trying not to make a sound, I pushed myself around and faced the case.

My heart beat as though I'd just run a race, my hands felt clammy, and my eyes were moist with tears. This little baby had stolen my childhood, my innocence, my hope for the future, and I hated him. But I had a strange yearning to know this child. I lifted my head and looked into the case, and my heart skipped a beat. There lay the smallest baby in the world.

There were tubes running from his nose, and monitor pads on his stomach and chest. His face was turned away from me. An intravenous tube ran into his right arm. A yellow light illuminated the incubator.

My God, he was a *lot* smaller than I expected, like a little doll. How could I hate such a small, innocent baby? He was just lying there, not moving at all. I looked at his fingers. They weren't webbed, and he only had ten. He also had ten perfect little toes. Slowly, I wheeled myself around to the other side of the incubator. I had to see his face.

It was the most peaceful sight imaginable. His tiny mouth looked like a line drawn on his face. His nose was like the prettiest button. He looked so pure. The image I'd had of an ugly, hateful creature growing inside of me shattered. This baby needed only a halo to be the perfect angel. I couldn't help but smile at his shiny little black curls.

How could something so good and pure and innocent come out of what Ralph did to me? My head felt light as I slipped my hands into the small openings of the incubator and allowed my fingers to touch him. When I touched his face, it felt like an electric current was burning my hands. My fingers traced the outline of his fragile body. I caressed his tiny hands. His fingers were so little, they were hardly there at all. The contact between my fingertips and his soft brown skin sent lightning through me. Taking his fingers in my hand, I concentrated on the texture of his soft delicate flesh, wanting to always remember it.

Then his fingers *moved*. They opened and closed in my hand. I gasped. Then his head moved. A small noise escaped his lips. I thought he was going to cry, but then he was silent again. His eyes were open. They were so glossy, a blackish grey, like smoke. He seemed to look right at me.

Gazing into his eyes, I felt as though I was falling into a trance. I was under his control. I tried to withdraw my hands from his private castle, but he wouldn't let me. His eyes demanded that I love him. The disgust I had felt when I came in melted away. I read a gentle language in his eyes; a kind language I had never heard before. He was telling me what I needed to hear: that he needed my love, that I had to be strong and survive, that he wouldn't allow me to be hurt again.

I wanted to hold him, to tell him I forgave him for being born. I wanted to protect him from my hate and anger, and from the truth — and the lies — beyond this room.

My trance was shattered when the nurse returned and briskly moved me away from the incubator.

"It's lunchtime."

I was speechless. I was not interested in lunch. The baby needed me to protect him from my parents' lies. I wanted to stay with him, to watch over him. But the nurse took me back to my room. First they'd taken me to see the baby when I didn't want to, and now they had taken me away from him when I wanted to stay. How could they just make decisions for me? And why couldn't I speak up and let them know I wasn't happy with what was going on?

The baby had all the answers, I thought. He knew none of this was my fault. He knew that I was innocent. He was my proof, my friend, my son.

"The doctor has put you on a liquid diet until you have a bowel movement," said the nurse.

I wanted to tell her that I didn't want to hear about any doctor's orders. But my feelings were being ignored. She helped me back into bed.

I couldn't sit up straight. I leaned forward, trying not to cry as a sharp pain shot through me, as if I was being ripped in half. Everything in the room started to look fuzzy. I sobbed to God to help me.

"I'll get you a painkiller," the nurse promised.

I wanted to feel my grandmother's arms around me. She was the one person who had always shown me love and affection. Whether I was getting into fights or doing well in school, she always had something good to say to me. I wanted to hear her sing to me. I longed for her to brush my hair with one hundred strokes and make it shine. I needed reassurance and encouragement, and I missed my grandmother dearly.

When at last I started to feel more comfortable, the nurse left. I felt a bit lightheaded from the pain killer, but little by little, I could feel my body relax. Feeling grateful, I made a mental note to thank the nurse for her help. I tried not to move, as I was afraid this would bring back the pain. I started to doze off again.

CHAPTER FIVE

I willed myself to stay awake, but my eyes closed anyway. As I drifted off, I wished I could be in control of my body and my thoughts. Then I was asleep, and Ralph took over my dreams. He entered the room slowly and stood before me, as plainly as he had that day in May. He was staring at me the way a man looks at a woman he wants. I couldn't move.

Standing directly over me, he started to stroke my hair. My heart beat quickly. He had a smile on his face. In my dream, I willed June to come home, but I knew she was going to be at work for at least another four hours. He knew that too. He also knew that later she would not believe me.

He looked so different now from the man I had met years ago, when June had first taken me to visit him in New York.

The night we got to New York, Ralph was taking June out for the night. I would be left alone in his apartment. I was very tired, so I was glad that I'd be getting some time to rest.

Ralph and June said goodbye to me and left, but then a few minutes later Ralph returned. He'd forgotten his keys. June was waiting for him downstairs.

He came over to the sofa bed and sat down beside me.

"I'm so happy to meet you finally," he said. "I've been trying to picture you in my mind for many years." He paused, then continued, "You know, Pet, of the four of you kids, I've always liked you the best, right from the start."

He leaned towards me. "Why don't you give your father a kiss?" he asked with a smile.

I leaned over and kissed him on the cheek.

"I want you to give me a *real* kiss," he said.

I didn't know what he meant. Before I could ask, he grabbed me by the back of my head and pulled my face close to his.

"I'll show you. After I've waited for so long to see you, I'm sure you can give me a better kiss than that."

Holding my head tightly between his hands, he brought his mouth down on mine and stuck his tongue in my mouth.

Confused, I closed my lips and pulled my head away. He stood up.

"We'll be spending a lot more time together soon," he said. "I'll teach you how to kiss me like a real father."

He tucked me in and left the apartment.

I wiped my lips, feeling a bit stupid. I had waited for so long to meet Ralph, and now I felt embarrassed to kiss him. I didn't want my new father to not like me over something as small as a kiss. I put aside the uneasy feeling in the pit of my stomach.

June had worked hard to bring us all together. I knew that Ralph was a big part of the reason why I was now living with my mother, and I was grateful.

Now, as he sat next to me in my dream, I felt the same kind of mixed emotions that I'd felt that night in New York. Ralph didn't look as though he was doing anything wrong; there wasn't a flicker of guilt on his face. Why hadn't anybody told me about this? Had my grandmother known that when I got a new father, this was going to be part of the package? I was angry at her for not preparing me. Though I hated what Ralph was doing, I believed that I must be doing something to bring it on. If I took control of the situation, I would be all right.

Ralph said that he loved me, and that he wanted to be a good father. He told me that it was a father's duty to teach his daughter all she needed to know about sex, so that her boyfriends and her husband wouldn't be disappointed. I believed him, but that didn't make me feel any better. I felt dirty. I didn't want to be touched, I didn't want to learn about sex, I just wanted to have a normal life like my friends. I wanted to be loved by my mother and Ralph, but the love he was giving me felt wrong. Nothing about it made me feel good. Nothing about my new family felt right any more.

Before Ralph joined us in Canada, June and I had had a lot of fun together. She would come into my room before she left for work and wake me up. She used to play-fight with Jerome and me for a long time before leaving for work. Sometimes, we would wake up in the morning to find that she had already left, but there would be lipstick on our faces where she had kissed us as we slept.

Sometimes we would go for walks together, or go shopping. We would hug each other all the way. Sometimes we would just hug and not talk. I felt proud to be with my mother, and I believed we would always love each other this way.

She would ask me over and over if I had missed her when I was living with my grandparents, and I could never tell her how much I had. Then she would ask me if I hated her for leaving me for so long. I didn't know how to explain that when it came to her, I had no time for anything like hate. She'd always been my hero.

But every time I tried to tell her I loved her, I'd get all choked up. I tried to call her Mother, but I just couldn't. She took this as proof that I didn't care. I wanted to call her Mother more than anything in the world — the words just refused to pass my lips. I couldn't explain it to her.

Sometimes June and I slept in the same bed. She would hug me and sometimes kiss me when she thought I was asleep. I was afraid to move because I didn't want her to stop. I felt safe. I enjoyed having a mother. I didn't realize how much I had missed her until I started seeing her every day. It felt good.

Then Ralph moved in with us. It was exciting to finally have him with us. He brought all the furniture from the apartment in New York, and he also brought me an organ and my own bedroom set.

Now my three brothers, my mother, my stepfather and I were all under the same roof. It was a safe feeling.

With Ralph there, and all that furniture in the apartment, we had to change our sleeping arrangements. Ralph and June took one bedroom, the three boys moved into my room, and I slept in the living room.

June was working two jobs and sometimes she came home pretty late. Not long after he arrived, Ralph started to come into the living room when June was away and I was sleeping on the sofa.

He was always polite. He would start off by asking me all kinds of questions. He said he wanted to catch up on what my life had been like when I lived with my grandparents in Trinidad. He asked about my schooling and even about how I felt about my mother.

Then he started to ask me personal questions that made me feel uncomfortable.

"Are you still a virgin?"

I found it strange that he would ask me such a question, as he knew very well that I was only thirteen. He wasn't even embarrassed.

"I know for a fact that you're no virgin," he announced one night. "I put my finger into your pussy last night and you don't feel the way a virgin is suppose to feel."

I was shocked. I knew that he shouldn't be talking to me like that. I started to feel uncomfortable when he sat near me at night. All of a sudden, I was afraid of him. He was still very polite and fatherly whenever June was around, and I couldn't understand why he changed so much when she was away.

He started to speak freely about sex when June was not around. He explained in detail many aspects of sex that I had never even imagined. Then he started to ask me about my feelings.

"Do you like sex?" he'd ask.

I felt very uncomfortable at his sudden curiosity about what I would or wouldn't like.

Then it happened. I was taking a nap one day in my brothers' room, as I sometimes did when no one else was there. I woke up when Ralph came in. I was shocked to see he was absolutely naked. With a strange look in his eyes, he sat down on the bed.

"I'm going to make you feel very good, Pet," he said in a low, husky voice. "I'm going to teach you how to make your husband happy."

My heart started pounding. He moved closer, staring at me as though he could look right through me. Horrified, I tried not to look at him. So slowly that I could hardly see him moving, he slid along the bed until he was sitting only inches away from me. Was this a joke? I prayed that he wouldn't do anything to hurt me, but I knew that it wasn't right for him to be here naked.

I tried to speak, but the words got stuck in my throat. Looking at him, I tried to figure out what was going through his mind. His face had no expression.

"You're so pretty, Pet," he said. "I didn't think that you were going to be so pretty." He started to stroke my cheeks.

"What are you doing with no clothes on?" I finally managed to ask.

"I'm going to make you a very happy girl."

"I want you to leave."

Touching my shoulders, he said, "I know you want it."

"Want what?"

He raised his voice. "Stop playing innocent, Pet. You know that you've wanted me to give it to you for a long time."

"Give me what?"

"Why don't you just behave yourself? I'm not going to hurt you."

He seemed to think I knew what he was talking about, and to have no idea how much he was frightening me.

"I mean it, Ralph. Get out of here."

"Why don't you stop the playing around?" he asked, looking me in the eye.

"I don't like this."

"You *will* like it. I'm going to take my time."

"I don't want you to do anything to me."

"Just relax." He pushed me down onto my back. "I'm going to make you feel very good."

I wanted to run away. I didn't know what was about to happen, but I knew enough to be scared.

Ralph started to rub his hand against my breast. The shock of it made me gasp. He squeezed my breast with both hands. Fear filled me, paralysing me. I couldn't even move my hands.

"I'm going to tell June if you don't stop," I said weakly.

"Go ahead. What do you think she'll do?" He squeezed my breast to the point of pain. "Maybe you'll be lucky and she'll send you back to live with your sick family in Trinidad." He looked at my face. "Would you like to go back to that shithole, with all those nasty things that your grandmother does?"

"I'll call the police," I said, desperate to scare him.

"Here," he said, grabbing the phone and handing it to me. "Go ahead. What are you waiting for?" He grinned mockingly.

Why was he giving me the phone? He wasn't even a bit afraid. It had to be a trap. He wanted me to do exactly what he said. I was too afraid to even touch the phone, let alone dial the number. He took back the phone, and lay back down.

"Now," he said. "Why don't you stop pretending like you don't want me to make love to you?"

"I don't."

"I'm going to make love to you like you never had it before. Have you ever had oral sex?"

"What?"

"Has anyone ever licked you down there? Would you like me to lick your pussy till you come in my mouth?" His hands began to touch my crotch as he spoke.

"No," I answered, my voice unsteady with fear. I felt like I was going to faint.

Ignoring my answer, he lowered his mouth and started to lick my breast. Then he moved up a bit and licked my ears. I hated the feel of his tongue against my skin. I wanted him to stop.

He got on top of me, lifted up my skirt and pulled off my underwear. Would June really send me back to Trinidad if I told her what he was doing?

I could feel his penis getting hard as he lay on top of me. I was afraid to look at him. Closing my eyes, I tried to pretend it was a dream. I could feel him rubbing his penis against my legs, and I wanted to scream. I thought that at any moment I might vomit from fear.

"I'm not going to hurt you, Pet. Don't worry. I'll be gentle," he whispered in my ear.

I tried not to cry. All the good feelings I had developed for him were quickly slipping away. He seemed to be feeling no guilt, no shame, about what he was doing. Why did he hate me so much?

I felt his penis up against my vagina, pushing hard. I bit down on my tongue as he entered me.

"You're so tight," he murmured, more to himself than to me. Then he moaned. I felt as though I was being split in two. I hated him. I wished I could hurt him as he was hurting me.

His tongue was playing with my ear. He started to move faster. The pain was unbearable, but my cries stuck in my throat.

Ralph was talking, but I couldn't make out what he was saying. I was swirling in a cloud of darkness. He started to fade. The last thing I remember is his voice saying the words I'll always hate: "I'll always love you, Pet."

I woke to find myself aching all over. It hadn't been a dream — Ralph really had raped me. I hated him for making me feel so dirty, for telling me that I liked it and wanted him to do it. Tears of pain and disgust flowed down my cheeks.

I felt something warm and wet on my legs, and looked down to see my own blood. He had left his male wetness in my vagina and along my legs. No fourteen-year-old could handle such shock and fear alone. I fell to my knees and cried out to God.

When I opened my eyes, Ralph was standing before me, still naked. His penis was limp, and the sweat on his bronze skin glowed in the sunlight. His brown eyes sparkled wickedly.

"It felt good, didn't it?"

From where I knelt on the floor, I looked up at him in disbelief. I felt as if I had just lost my soul, and he was acting as if he had done nothing wrong. I wondered for a moment whether I was taking this all wrong.

Without waiting for my reply, he walked away and went to the bathroom. I wanted to disappear.

During the rape I had tried to pretend that it wasn't really happening. Now, as I saw him leave the bathroom fully dressed, I wanted to kill him. I had no doubt that he had brutalized me; my aching body, and the slime of his ejaculation, told me so in no uncertain terms.

In the bathroom, I sat down on the toilet and tried to wipe off the blood and semen. I had never seen semen up close, but I was sure that this was what the strange-smelling goo was. It was drying on my legs — no matter how hard I wiped, it would not come off.

I turned on the shower and stepped in, then stripped off my few remaining clothes, grabbed the soap and started to roughly scrub myself. I bit my tongue as I started to wash between my legs. The soap and the water brought with them an agonizing burning. The burning brought such a force to my anger that I thought it would destroy me. But I was also starting to feel guilty. What had I done to make Ralph believe I wanted him to do this? He'd said it was my fault. I tried to think whether I'd ever said I wanted sex. How could I have said such a thing and not remember it?

I couldn't soap away the dirty feeling that filled me. Everything had happened so fast, my head was spinning. I wanted things to slow down so that I could think about what to do. I prayed for June to come home. I longed for my grandmother. I wanted someone to tell me that everything would be all right.

CHAPTER SIX

I went back to the room where I had been violated, and was surprised to find that the sheet with the blood and semen had vanished. I took out my diary and lay down on the bed. I felt different.

As I'd passed the mirror along the wall in the bedroom, I couldn't see any bruises on my body, but I knew they were there. I could feel them. If my skin was not such a dark shade of brown, I'd have been covered in black and blue spots, but except for a few red blotches here and there, I looked like any Black girl of fourteen.

Things were going to be different. I wasn't going to be nice any more. I wanted to be bad, so bad that everyone would leave me alone.

I started to write. First I wrote the date: May 13, 1982. I made a note in my diary to always hate May 13. The time was now eleven minutes before three o'clock, so I figured that the whole thing must have taken about thirty minutes.

Writing was the only thing I really enjoyed doing. It had always made me feel good. But for some reason writing wasn't working today. I couldn't think clearly. I tossed the diary across the bed, and sat and cried. The ache between my legs got worse. I was ashamed to leave the room.

I had believed that Ralph loved me. He was always willing to help with my school work, and he had said many times that he wished I was his biological daughter. I cooked when I was supposed to, did the laundry and cleaned the house. I was getting very good grades. For the life of me, I just couldn't figure out what I had done wrong. After I had tried so hard to be good and to be loved, he had hurt me terribly. I was never going to forgive him.

When June came home that night, I was unusually eager to see her. I wanted to tell her about what Ralph had done. I tried to think of a way to tell her that wouldn't sound stupid. I was waiting when she walked in the door.

"Can I speak to you for a minute please?" I asked.

"Is that the only thing you could find to say? I haven't even walked into the apartment properly, and you're already starting. Can't you even say good evening?"

Her hair was combed back as usual, and her tall dark frame glided across the apartment with ease. She strode past me and into their room. I was about to follow her when Ralph brushed past me and called out that he needed to speak to her.

I sat down in the living room, still shaking from what had happened earlier. A few minutes later, June came out of the bedroom and stormed towards me. I could see the anger in her deep brown eyes.

"Why did you tell Ralph that when he was in New York I was sleeping around with someone?"

In minutes, Ralph had managed to turn June against me. He knew I was planning to tell her about what he had done. Now, I was so stunned, I couldn't get any words out. He was nowhere in sight.

Then June punched me in the head. I felt my neck snap backwards.

"He's just saying that because he knew I was going to tell you what he did to me today!" I screamed.

"It's not enough for you to go around telling lies about me, you have to make up lies about Ralph too. You don't appreciate anything we've done for you!"

"He's lying. *He* won't leave *me* alone. He didn't want me to tell you that he forced me to have sex with him today!"

She ignored this. "You think you're a fucking woman in this house!" She punched me again, in the side of the head. I held up my hand to block the next blow.

"And you want to hit me, too?" she screamed, punching me harder.

In tears, I cried, "I'm not trying to fight you!"

"So you want to hit your mother, do you?"

She pushed me down on the floor. As I fell, I saw Ralph standing in the corner, watching my mother beat me. There was no expression on his face. He just stood there staring.

June was sitting on me, hitting me again and again. I twisted around, trying to get her off me. I was losing strength.

"You want to fight, do you?" she said again.

"It's your husband who had sex with me. Why are you hitting *me?*" I yelled.

"So now Ralph's having sex with you?" She hit me in the head, so hard that I saw stars. "Just because he told me about your lies, you want to blame him for something. Do you know how much work he had to do just to bring you here to Canada?" Her voice was starting to crack. "You're so fucking ungrateful. This is the thanks we get for everything that we did for you!" She swung a punch that caught me in the right eye. "I should have left you with your grandmother. All you ever talk about is her. Maybe you should go back, if you were so happy there. If you think that you came all the way to Canada to break up my marriage, you've got another think coming."

She got up and went back into her room, slamming the door. I lay on the floor, where she left me. After a few minutes, I got up. My legs were trembling. I wanted to run and hide.

I went to my room. As I lay down, I heard her say, "You had better not come out of that room if you know what's good for you, Pet."

I could hear Ralph telling her I wanted to break up their marriage.

"She doesn't like me, June."

I wished he was dead.

Then I thought of Paula, my mother's friend. She used to look after us kids when June went to visit Ralph in New York. Paula had told me that if I ever needed to talk, I could come over. Her home was kind of far away, but I decided to go anyway. I needed to talk to someone, but I would wait until things had settled down a bit before I went.

Paula lived alone with her only son. She was nice to us. When we stayed with her, she used to make us her special pancakes. When my period had first started, a few months earlier, I had been staying at her house. I was scared when I woke up and found my nightclothes were wet with blood. I knocked on Paula's bedroom door, and she helped me to clean up and explained what I was going through. She showed me how to use a maxi pad and talked about the birds and the bees. She seemed almost excited about the whole thing, and told me that I was now a young woman. Except for a few cramps, I didn't feel any different, but I was happy that Paula thought I was almost grown up. She let me sleep in her room that night.

Paula always tried to persuade me to call June Mother. She told me that when I refused, I was hurting June's feelings. I felt really bad, but I still couldn't do it. It was just too hard.

Now, lying in bed, I decided that Paula was the best person to talk to. Once Paula knew, she would make my mother see that what Ralph did was wrong.

June had never before hit me like she had today. I was still in shock. I had never seen her so upset. I couldn't understand why she had refused to listen to me. I wanted to prove to her that I wasn't trying to hurt her. I wanted her to know what Ralph had done to me, and I wanted her to keep him from ever doing it again.

My brothers had come home, and they sat in the living room watching TV. None of them came in to see what was wrong or to ask me if I was all right. Though I prayed I was wrong, it seemed to me like something strange was happening to my family, and things were only going to get worse from now on.

It was almost eleven that night when I slipped out of the bedroom window and headed for Paula's place. It was dark and very humid. I had managed to twist my ankle, making walking uncomfortable. But the peace and silence soothed me. I felt safe knowing no one could see me; I felt like anyone who looked at me would know what had happened to me, and would blame me for it.

I stood in the hallway of Paula's apartment building, in front of her door, for a couple of minutes before I knocked. She answered immediately.

"Pet! What the hell are you doing out at this time?"

"I need to talk to you."

"Come on inside." She looked out into the hallway. "Where's June?"

"She's at home. She doesn't know I'm here." I went into the living room. She followed and sat down next to me on the sofa.

"You shouldn't be out by yourself so late."

"I had to wait until everyone was asleep."

Paula sat and looked at me for a few minutes without saying anything. Finally she said, "Why don't you tell me why you've snuck all the way down here by yourself?"

I was glad to see Paula, but I was starting to feel uneasy about what I had to tell her. I took a couple of deep breaths and tried not to cry. The day was still fresh in my mind, but I'd had a chance to do some thinking during the walk to her place. I realized that June's reaction had hurt me even more than what Ralph had done. Ralph had known all along that she wouldn't listen to me. When he had offered me the phone, he had known that I wouldn't call the police.

I didn't tell Paula a whole lot. She wasn't going to be able to be much help. I told her that I was having some problems with Ralph, and that my mother was not listening to me. When I left, I promised her I'd make it home safely.

When I got home, June was sitting in the living room waiting for me. Paula had called her and told her of my visit.

"What the hell is your problem?" she demanded.

I couldn't believe it. I'd messed up again.

"Did you ask to leave this house?"

I wanted to shrink away. The last thing I wanted was more of what had happened earlier that evening.

"You just won't stop until you've broken up my marriage, will you?"

"I didn't do anything wrong."

"What gives you the right to go to my friend and tell her all this garbage? You just can't behave yourself for once, can you?"

"Well, if you'd listen to me, I wouldn't have to go around telling anyone anything," I said quietly. I knew how that statement would go over, but I didn't care. I was tired of always having to defend myself.

"I should have left your black ass in Trinidad with your fucking grandmother! You think she's perfect? Well, for your information, I didn't have such an easy life with her. Why don't you go back and live with her if you're so unhappy here? I know that you keep doing this to get back at me for leaving you. Well, you don't know how hard it was for me to get you and your brother up here ... I should have left you with her when I had the chance." With that, she went back to her room.

CHAPTER SEVEN

When I got up the next morning, both June and Ralph had already left. My brothers had gone to school. I was happy to be alone. I sat in bed for a while, wondering if what had happened the day before had been a dream. When I sat up to reach for my diary, though, I knew it was no dream. The pain in my head from the beating was very real.

I sat through most of my morning classes at Winchester Public School in a daze, trying to work out exactly what had happened, and what I should do.

Most of my lower body was very sore. It burned when I used the toilet.

After school, I walked home with my friend Trish. Although Trish was White and I was Black, we had become friends almost as soon as we met. That we weren't of the same race didn't seem to matter at all; as a matter of fact, I thought it made our friendship more interesting. I'd only been in Canada for two years, and I learned a lot about this country from Trish. And she was interested in my life in Trinidad, which I thought was pretty neat. Trish was a few months older than me, but she was so petite that no one ever guessed this.

Trish and I stopped at a park on our way to her house, and I decided to tell her what had happened. I was so scared I didn't know where to start.

"I mean it, Trish. Don't tell *anybody*."

"What are you going to do?"

"I can't do anything."

I was too ashamed to tell her that my mother didn't want to do anything about it, so I said that my mother didn't believe me. From that day on, every time Ralph touched me in a sexual way, I confided in Trish. For both of us, it was hard to deal with, but I was glad that someone believed me. Trish and I became inseparable.

In July of 1982 I started to feel awfully sick. I was throwing up almost daily, sometimes three or four times a day. One afternoon during the second week in July, June came home from work while I was in the bathroom,throwing up.

"What's wrong with you?"

"I keep getting sick to my stomach. It's been going on for a while now."

"What colour is it?"

"Kind of yellowish-brownish."

"As far as I know, people only throw up like that when they're pregnant."

The next day, she told me I had an appointment with Dr. Stevenson, our family doctor. Not knowing what to expect, I went with her to his office, only one block away from our apartment. I'd told Dr. Stevenson before about what Ralph was doing to me. He had called June after I left his office, and told her that I'd been making up stories about my stepfather. I'd gotten into a lot of trouble that day.

"Hello, Vanessa. Your mother says that you have an upset stomach."

As Dr. Stevenson examined me, I kept thinking about what my mother had told him.

"If I'm pregnant, it's Ralph who did it, you know," I blurted out. "He's a fucking black bitch and I hate his ass."

"Now, Vanessa, you know your mother and stepfather love you a lot. It's not easy for them when you go around saying things like that."

I hated it when adults acted like they were concerned about you, when all they really cared about was protecting each other. "You're all the same! Just because they're adults, you think they can do no wrong. Someday I'm going to make all of you see that he's been forcing me to have sex with him. I hate sex and I hate him!" I slid off the examination table.

"It looks like you have a bit of an upset stomach. You may have some excess acid in your digestive system. I'll give you a prescription for some pills which should help," said Dr. Stevenson. "I'll call your mother and let her know that you're all right."

September rolled around, and Trish and I started high school. We also joined the Air Force as cadets. There were only two other Black people at the weekly meetings — a cadet named Tom, and our sergeant, Charles. Charles was pretty cool. He used to call us, and sometimes he'd arrange rides for us to and from meetings. Sometimes when meetings went on until after ten, he'd walk us home, so that we didn't have to walk home alone. He spoke to us like we were people.

Charles and I talked a lot about things that involved Black people in general. I was still having a hard time figuring out the differences between the Black folks back in Trinidad and the ones here in Canada. "Do you think people listen to White folks more than to us, Charles?" I asked one night.

"What you mean?"

"Like if I was White and I had a problem, do you think people might help me?"

"I don't think it really makes a difference. I *hope* it don't make a difference."

"Do you think Canada is a White man's place, and if you're not White you don't really count?"

"I hope not."

"But I hardly ever see Black folks sticking up for each other. You know Trish's mother would stick up for her anytime. My mother seems to be on a different wavelength. Why don't Black people just start liking each other?"

"I don't have the answers, I'm afraid."

"Black people don't look like they're ever going to fight together. And it looks to me like we won't ever win if we don't ever fight. Hardly any White people stand up for us. It seems to me like we'd better stand up for each other and get rid of those Black asses who give us a bad name and a bad rap. If we let them know they're messing up our future and make them shape up, maybe we'll have a chance to be really free as Black people."

It seemed to me that Black folks were more united in Trinidad than here. In school, I saw Black kids forming cliques. If they didn't want you in, you stayed out, even if you were blacker than night. I had never seen that happen in Trinidad. I figured that if Black folks didn't like Black folks, no wonder White folks didn't know how to feel about us. We weren't even setting good examples for ourselves, much less for our children and for others.

CHAPTER EIGHT

Once we moved into Ontario Housing, I started going across the street to the park when I wanted time alone. My brothers were making friends of their own and were hardly ever around. Ralph was still unemployed. He spent a lot of time reading newspapers and watching television.

One morning in September, I was on my way out of the house when June asked, "Pet, you're not pregnant, are you?"

Shocked, I turned to face her. "*What?*"

"You look like you're putting on some weight. Are you sure you haven't been having sex with anyone?" She was watching me closely. I despised her.

"The only man I've been having sex with is your husband, but you keep telling me that's all a lie. So I guess I'm not having sex. Therefore, I can't very well be pregnant, can I?" At this point I didn't care if she hit me.

"Who the hell do you think you're talking to? I'm not your friend. You think you can just say anything you want to in this house?"

I *was* getting fat. Ralph had forced himself on me five times. My body didn't feel right, but I couldn't bring myself to think that I might be pregnant. It was as if I couldn't be pregnant if I refused to believe it. But now that June had brought it up, I was afraid it might be true.

"I'm calling Dr. Stevenson. We're going to see once and for all." She picked up the phone.

"I have to meet Trish at the library," I said. I didn't want to see Dr. Stevenson again — I knew that he was going to take my mother's side.

"Get your coat," June said. "We've got an appointment."

Tears formed in my eyes. "What's the use, when you never believe anything I tell you anyway?"

"You don't have a choice, Pet."

When we got to Dr. Stevenson's office, his assistant told me to undress and sit on the examination table. My mother talked to the doctor for a few minutes while I waited. Then Dr. Stevenson came into the examination room and started to feel my abdomen. It hurt when he pressed down on my belly. Each time he squeezed one particular area, I felt like I was out of breath.

Although he didn't look at me, I could see the expression on his face change. I knew what that meant.

"Have you felt any movement?" he asked.

"Only the gas that you gave me the acid pills for," I answered.

"This is not funny, Vanessa."

"Who fucking said anything about anything being funny?"

"What do you think your mother would say if she could hear you?"

"Does you really think I *care* what June or Ralph or anyone else has to say?" I screamed. "*I'm* the one that has to live with all this. Do any of you know how fucking screwed up my head is with all this shit?"

"Well, you certainly are pregnant," Dr. Stevenson said, taking off his gloves and motioning for me to get dressed. "What do you plan to do about it?"

I glared at him.

"What do you mean, what am I going to do about it?"

"You have a lot to consider. You're very young. Not a lot of fourteen-year-olds have children. It's a big responsibility."

He opened the door to the examination room and let my mother in.

"You were right, June. It looks like she's about five months into the pregnancy."

June looked at me. "What are you planning to do?"

"Why are you asking me?" I said, looking her in the eye. "You wouldn't believe me when I tried to tell you that your husband was forcing me to have sex with him. Why don't you ask Ralph what *he's* going to do about this?"

"Who is the father?"

I wondered whether my mother had heard anything I had said over the past several months.

"Are you crazy?" I gasped.

"We'll talk about this when we get home."

"Unfortunately, June," said Dr. Stevenson, "it's a bit late for an abortion." He looked at me. "You're lucky to have such understanding parents."

"I'm *lucky*? I'm lucky to have a father who thinks he can get away with fucking me whenever he feels like it?"

How could they both be so stupid?

"Thanks, Dr. Stevenson," June said. "I appreciate you taking the time to see us on such short notice."

"Any time. Let me know what you're going to do."

During the trip home, June ignored me, and I had no problem with that. When we got in, I went to my room and sat on the bed. I wanted to call Trish and tell her about what had just happened, but June was on the phone. She called out to me to pick up the extension. I came out of my room, but when I realized it was Paula she was talking to, I wanted to run back in and shut the door. Since that night when I confided in her and she squealed on me, I no longer trusted Paula. But I knew that if I didn't talk to her, that would be something else to get yelled at for.

"Hello, Paula," I said. I had stopped calling her Aunt. June had always insisted that it was disrespectful to call adults by their first names; we had to call her friends Aunt. It had never bothered me before, but after what Paula had done I refused to call her Aunt ever again.

"Your mother tells me that you just found out you're pregnant," Paula said.

"I guess so."

"Pet, you have to get serious about this whole thing now."

"I *am* serious. What makes you think I'm not?"

"You have to stop giving your mother such a hard time."

It was taking Paula a long time to get to the point, and I was glad the conversation was making her so uncomfortable.

"I didn't know that I was giving her so much trouble," I said.

"Well, she has an awful lot to deal with. You're not making things any easier for her by being rude and not listening."

I used to value Paula's pep talks. Now, listening to her made me feel sick.

"Well, it was nice talking to you again. I have to go," I said, cutting her off. I put the phone down and went back to my room.

I told Trish that I was pregnant soon after I found out. She was almost as afraid as I was.

I wished that this wasn't happening so soon after I started at my new school. I wouldn't be able to hide my situation for much longer. I was already having a hard time fitting into some of my clothes, and I knew that sooner or later everyone in my school would know and would laugh at me. In a way it would be a relief when it was no longer a secret. But I was sure that everyone would blame me and, as usual, Ralph would look completely innocent.

The next three months dragged on and on. June and I talked to each other only when it was absolutely necessary. My brothers hardly talked to me at all. Jerome and I talked to each other only when we were alone. I understood why he was ignoring me: if he had been seen to be on my side, he would have been singled out as a traitor.

When June confirmed to the others that I was pregnant, everything changed. My brothers were suddenly given a lot more freedom than they were used to. Before my pregnancy, Jerome and I had been responsible for cleaning the house, cooking and tidying up after meals and doing the laundry. Now, I was solely responsible for these chores. Before, my brothers and I used to sit around and talk about how stupid June was to always be trailing along after Ralph. We had even talked about hurting Ralph if he ever touched any of us again. Now, Ralph played basketball with them after school, and at times I could hear them laughing loudly at his jokes.

Before my pregnancy, Jerome had been picked on and treated as an outcast. Now, he was liked and included in things. We were no longer as close as we had been when we lived in Trinidad. I was lonely and I missed talking to him.

I stayed in my room most of the time, coming down to the kitchen to do the dishes only long after dark when I was sure everyone was asleep. I would mop the kitchen floor, then get some of my homework done at the kitchen table.

June tried to blame Charles for making me pregnant. It was really embarrassing. She called the Squadron and complained to Charles's supervisor. I found out afterwards, from Trish, that Charles was questioned about my pregnancy. I hoped he wouldn't mention my mother's allegations to my friends in the Air Cadets; I didn't want them to know that I was pregnant. I was especially worried that they would think that I'd put my mother up to it. But Charles never mentioned it to anyone. He proved to be a true friend. He understood when I told him I couldn't be in the Air Cadets any more.

I would have liked for Charles to have been the baby's father. But then, I would have liked for just about anyone but my stepfather to have been Christopher's father.

I had started wearing larger sweaters to school. Well ... *stretched* sweaters, actually. I got this brilliant idea one day while I was doing laundry. By accident I washed my sweaters in hot water. When I took them out, they were all stretched beyond belief. At first I laid them out to dry on a table and tried to pull them back into shape. Then it came to me: why not wear them as if they were *meant* to be big? So I did.

Trish and I were spending a lot of time together. Sometimes we talked about the baby. We had part-time jobs selling newspapers over the phone. It was nice getting paid for being away from home. I gave June some of the money I made. Sometimes she asked me to pick up odds and ends at the grocery — one of those rare times we actually spoke to each other.

During Christmas week, June threw a party for some of her close friends. At the party, June and Ralph ignored me, and I ignored them. But I heard the remarks their friends made, and I saw them looking at me with shame and disgust when they thought I wouldn't notice.

Then one day in January, the pain in my abdomen began. Ralph and I had an argument; I was yelling at him about how sick he was. June sent me to my room and told me to stay there or she'd be forced to take me out of this world as quickly as she'd brought me into it. I tried to tell her about the cramps in my belly, but as usual she listened to Ralph. They left me in my room to deal with the pain on my own. It was almost two days before I was forced to ask her for help.

CHAPTER NINE

When finally I woke from a very troubled sleep, I was looking forward to seeing my baby again. I had new hope. If this baby, conceived in such a hateful manner, could be pure and innocent, maybe some of the other problems in my life could also turn out okay. But nobody came to take me to see him. Instead, I was visited by a woman I hadn't met before.

"I'm the hospital's grief counsellor. I'm here to help you learn some new skills that will enable you to deal with your loss," she said.

"What loss?" I was still tired. My eyes felt heavy from all the medication.

"I'm sorry. I thought you knew."

"Knew what?"

"I thought you knew your baby passed away."

I pulled myself to a sitting position. A sharp pain shot through me. "What do you mean my baby passed away?"

"Vanessa, your son died a few hours ago."

She must be making a mistake, I thought. I'd seen him just a little while ago, and he looked so peaceful. How could he die? He wouldn't do that to me. He was going to help me prove to everyone that I wasn't a bad person.

"Are you all right?"

"There must be a mistake," I said, struggling to keep from raising my voice.

"Your mother was here. She's making the arrangements for the funeral."

I didn't want to hear about the funeral. I didn't want to hear anything about Christopher Lee not being alive.

"I know that this is hard for you. You have to be strong and try not to think about it. You need your strength to recover from your operation. You underwent major surgery this morning."

I wondered whether June had put her up to this. After all she'd done to hurt me over the past few months, I wouldn't have put it past her. I could feel my hate and anger start to flare up again. I snapped at the counsellor, "Don't tell me what to do and don't tell me what to think!"

"I'm here to see if there is anything that I can do for you."

"I don't want you to do anything for me."

"It's my job to speak to mothers who have lost their babies. You're very young, and I want to help you deal with all the emotions that come with losing a child."

"I'm not a normal young mother," I said, starting to cry again. "I'm not interested in you or what you have to say. I'm not interested in what you normally do. I just want to see my baby." I would never believe he was dead unless I could see for myself.

How could he have died without saying goodbye to me? He wasn't like everyone else. He cared about me. I wanted him to stay with me and help me deal with the world. I wanted to hold him, just to feel him in my arms. While I was pregnant, I had prayed for the baby I was carrying to die, but that was because I thought he was going to be a monster. Why did God have to answer my prayers *now*? He never had before.

"Are you all right, Vanessa?"

"I want to see my baby."

"He's dead," she said gently.

"I want to see my *baby*."

"Vanessa." She leaned closer to me. "Your baby died a few hours ago."

"Where's the doctor?"

"He'll be in to see you in the morning."

"Where's my mother?"

"I don't know. I only met with her for a short time. I believe she's taking care of the funeral arrangements."

"I don't believe you."

"It's the truth."

"Then why didn't anyone tell me?"

She looked sad. "I don't know."

After a minute or two, I asked, "What are they going to do with him?"

"He's going to be buried. He was signed over to your mother. The hospital isn't responsible for looking after funeral arrangements."

"When can I see him?"

"That's not up to me. I don't think that you'll be allowed to, not in your condition."

She was answering me without making me feel stupid for asking. I decided that she had to be telling me the truth.

"When did it happen?" I asked. Maybe they had gotten my baby mixed up with someone else's.

"As far as I know, about three hours ago."

"I just saw him about three hours ago!"

"It must have happened just after you left."

"Why did it happen?"

"I'm not sure. I heard something about your baby being transferred to the Sick Children's Hospital. I know that he was premature. This hospital isn't equipped for those births. I guess by the time they were able to make the arrangements to move him, it was too late." There was sadness in her voice.

Then she said, "I have to get going. If you need anything, you can reach me through the hospital's grief program. I hope that everything works out for you." She got up to leave. "Good luck, Vanessa."

As usual, I was left with more questions than answers.

The more I cried, the more I hurt, physically and emotionally. I called for a nurse three times over the next two hours. They kept telling me that they'd send someone soon. Finally, a nurse arrived and gave me a needle, saying, "This will help ease the discomfort."

"Could you tell me what is happening with my baby?"

"I just came on shift. I only take care of medication. You'd have to ask the head nurse."

The nurse left my side, and went to attend to the woman in the next bed.

"When is the head nurse coming?" I asked.

"She's around somewhere. A hospital is a very busy place, you know. You're not the only patient who wants to see a nurse."

"Does anyone else know anything about my baby?"

"I told you, the nurse in charge will see you as soon as she has time." As she was leaving the room, she stopped in the doorway, then turned back to me and said, "Please remember that the nurse's call button is for use only in emergencies."

I tried to turn on my side, but the pain was too severe. Somehow, I managed to fall asleep anyway. When I woke up, my face was still moist from tears. Beside my bed there was a box of chocolates and a new nightgown.

Seeing the puzzled look on my face, the woman in the next bed told me that my mother had come by for a visit. She had only stayed for a short while and had left no message.

"You poor thing," said my roommate.

"What did she say to you?"

"Nothing. But I did hear from the nursery that your baby died. I lost my first-born too. I know what you're going through."

"What else did you hear?"

"Only that you had a little boy. I just had a boy. He weighs six pounds and two ounces. Don't worry. With time you learn to go on. You're still young. You have lots of time to have more children."

"No one is telling me anything."

"I know how it is. Everyone is always so busy here." She hesitated. "Do you mind if I ask you how old you are?"

I thought for a moment before answering. A lot of people were shocked at how young I was, so I decided not to tell her the truth. I was going to be fifteen in less than a month. I added one more year.

"I'm sixteen."

"You're so young! This must be an awful experience for you," she exclaimed. "Are you going to get married to the baby's father?"

How was I supposed to explain to a complete stranger that I'd just had a baby for my stepfather?

"No," I answered.

"It's not because of the baby's death, is it?"

"No."

"That's too bad. Well, I hope everything works out for the best," she said, and picked up a magazine she had on her bed.

The doctor visited me the next day, to check my stitches, but he said nothing about the baby. Later in the day, June came to see me. She told me right away that she couldn't stay long. And she told me that when I returned home, I would be expected to stick to the rules. I had actually felt glad to see her, hoping she would tell me more about the baby, but she said nothing about him. It was clear that we would not be discussing him.

We hadn't been on good terms for a long time, but that day — January 24, 1983 — I finally lost her. My mother was a stranger to me.

CHAPTER TEN

had been home from the hospital for less than a week, and I was still having a hard time walking. The scar from the C-section was about four and a half inches long. It started at my belly button and went straight down to my pubic hair. It was a while before I was actually able to look at it. The first time was on February 12th, the day before my fifteenth birthday. I had just taken a shower. I stood in front of the mirror in my bedroom and took off the towel. It was difficult to stand up straight; my stomach muscles were still weak, and I felt like something was pulling and tugging at my intestines every time I stood up. I was afraid to do the exercises that the nurse had shown me. I had this image of the stitches bursting and my guts spilling out on the floor.

As I stood there, looking at the long scar that would always remind me my baby was real, Ralph came into my room. Startled, I reached for my towel and covered myself.

"That was a beautiful baby we created together," he said.

He had never before acknowledged the baby or that it was his. I wanted to hit him. "I'm getting dressed," I said coldly.

"Why are you acting like such a bitch? You know that I love you, Pet. Are you all right?"

"Fuck you!" I yelled.

Ignoring this, he came closer, and touched my face.

"Don't fucking touch me! You're a piece of shit and one day I'll watch you cry as surely as you keep me crying."

"Calm down," he said, in a soft voice.

"Get out of my room!"

I was exhausted, and this confrontation was the last thing I wanted. Starting to turn away, I felt the sting of his hand across my face.

"What did you do that for?"

"Don't be stupid! After all that I've done for you, you're acting like a spoiled brat."

"You've never done anything for me!"

"You don't appreciate anything. If it wasn't for me, your mother would have left you with your grandmother. You still don't know how lucky you are."

My mouth fell open. How could he believe what he was saying — or expect me to believe it?

"Since you got pregnant, you think you're an adult. All that foul language. You'd better watch your mouth if you know what's good for you."

I felt like showing him just how nasty my mouth could be. I wasn't afraid of him any more. Losing Christopher had given me the will to hurt Ralph and June. I had been in trouble for so long that I really didn't care if I got into more. At least, I didn't think I cared.

He left, and I closed the door and pushed the dresser in front of it. My whole body was shaking. I was angry at myself for letting him get to me.

I walked back over to the mirror and took my towel off again. I couldn't believe what I saw. Staring back at me was a young woman, about twenty-five pounds heavier than I had been one year ago. There were dark patches on her arms and legs, and strange-looking stretch marks on her arms, shoulders and stomach. I looked at her face. Her eyes were deep and hollow, with no softness in them. Her cheeks were still plump, but there were dark shadows under her eyes. Her breasts were about twice the size mine used to be.

I looked at the scar on my stomach again. It was so long. I touched it and it felt tender.

I hated this body. I was going to be fifteen the next day, but I didn't feel like a fifteen-year-old girl. I felt cheap and ugly. I wanted to disappear.

A lot had changed while I was in the hospital. My brothers were never around, and Jerome had made his own friends. A lot of the guys he hung out with now were into stealing, and they were no strangers to the police. I knew that our friendship would never be the same. Our innocence had been taken, mine by Ralph's sexual assaults, and Jerome's by watching me get hurt. Jerome never asked me about the baby and I never told him.

I got dressed and went downstairs to the TV room. Jerome had just come home, and I heard Ralph yelling at him to do his homework.

"I don't have any," said Jerome, heading upstairs to his room.

"So you're starting to follow in your sister's footsteps, are you?" yelled Ralph. "All of a sudden you think you're a man. You can get the hell out of my house if you think you're a man here! You're going to turn out just as stupid as your father!"

"Why don't you just leave him alone?" I jumped in.

Ralph turned to look at me standing at the foot of the stairs. "So you think you're bad, do you?"

"He *said* that he didn't have any homework."

"You think that now you've had a child that means you're a woman?" he snapped. He rushed at me, his hand balled into a fist. I raised my hand to block the blow, but his fist slammed into my head.

"So you want to fight, do you?"

"Don't touch me!"

"I'm your father, and I'll touch you whenever the hell I feel like it."

"You're not my father!"

He hit me a second time. I tried to keep my balance. The force of the blow made my eyes water.

"After everything I've done for you, this is all you can do!"

He drew back to hit me a third time, but I shoved past him and started to run up the stairs. Just when I thought I was free, he grabbed the cable converter and threw it at me. It hit me in the head, and I felt dizzy. Without thinking, I picked it up and threw it back at him. I missed. He came at me, and I knew he wasn't going to let me get away with throwing it at him.

"I'll fucking kill you!" he screamed.

His eyes were bright red, and for the first time I saw his hatred of me in his face.

"Do you think you can come into my house and do whatever the hell you want?"

I ran up the stairs, my stomach aching from the operation. Before I reached the top, he hit me with the converter again. He was catching up to me. I ran into my room and tried to close the door, but he pushed his way in.

He grabbed me by the hair and punched me in the head, over and over. My vision went blurry. Then he punched me in the stomach, where the scar was. The fresh pain was so intense that I fell to the floor. I was sure that he was going to punch me again when the phone began to ring.

"Don't you ever talk back to me again," he said as he walked out of my room.

I thought of calling June and telling her what just happened, but then I remembered what she had done when I tried to tell her that Ralph raped me, and I knew I couldn't. My body felt hot all over from the blows. I wondered if the stitches had burst.

I threw myself onto my bed and cried, trying to relieve the pain by rocking back and forth. I was beginning to wonder whether I was crazy. Maybe it was all in my head. Was the pain I felt real? Was the baby real? Maybe it was all in my head. I didn't know any more. Everything was blurry. Nothing made sense.

Ralph was talking to June on the phone, saying something about me. I tried to make out what he was saying.

"You'd better do something about that girl, June. Either she leaves or I leave. I'm not going to live in the same house with her for much longer," I heard him say. "She lashed out at me today. She wanted to fight. When I told her to settle down, she broke the converter for the television. She went up to her room and slammed the door." He paused, listening to June. Then he said, "Just hurry up and do something. I can't live like this any more, June. You know she won't be happy until she succeeds in breaking up our marriage." It was so easy for him to convince her. I hadn't even had a chance to speak to her, and I'd already lost.

"She's your daughter, you deal with her. I'm not going to let her drive me crazy. She's already told all kinds of lies about me. I'll be in our room when you get here."

June came home a short time later. I was still holding on to a small hope that sooner or later she'd believe me, that she'd help me. That was all that kept me from hating her as much as I hated Ralph.

June and I still weren't speaking much. She said nothing about the baby and showed no interest in my physical and emotional health.

She went into her room and spoke to Ralph, then came into my room. She sat down on my bed and said nothing for a few seconds. I could see she was angry.

"What the fuck is the matter with you?" she said finally.

I'd never really gotten used to hearing her swear. The first time she'd sworn at me was after Ralph raped me for the first time.
"What is your problem, Pet? Why can't you just try not to cause so much trouble?"

"Why don't you ever ask me anything? You always just assume that I'm lying and Ralph's telling the truth. Why do you always believe everything he says?"

I was crying again. Lately, everything was making me cry.

She said, "You always have an excuse for everything. Why don't you just stop? I work hard all day and I can't even come home to a decent, quiet evening. You're always doing something stupid."

"Why don't you believe me when I try to tell you what he's doing?" I pleaded. "He tries to have sex with me every time you go to work."

June got up to leave. "Why don't you just stop? You've already caused so much trouble. Are you so jealous of me that you have to keep up these stupid stories about Ralph? When are you going to stop trying to break up my marriage? What makes you think that Ralph would want to have sex with you when he has me?"

Striding towards the door, she stopped and turned back to me. "How many men do you think would marry a woman with four kids and treat them like his own? You don't know how lucky you are."

"I don't see what makes me so lucky when my stepfather wants to have sex with me all the time. He's married to my mother, not to me," I said.

To my surprise, she left without responding. I'd seen a new look in her eyes; I think it was fatigue. Like she was getting tired of the same old arguments.

I decided to go for a walk. On my way out I passed Ralph, who was sitting at the kitchen table with a glass of vodka in his hand. He looked into my eyes, as if to say, *you lose.*

"You're such a liar," I said, walking past him.

He just smiled at me. I felt disgusted. I stopped and said to him, "Don't think that you're going to get away with all of this. One of these days I'm going to make sure that you pay for it. I'll make sure that you pay for everything."

"Don't make threats that you can't keep."

At this point June walked into the kitchen.

"Watch your mouth, Pet," she said.

"Why don't you tell him to keep his hands off me?"

She sat down at the table. I pulled out a chair and sat down opposite her, challenging her in front of Ralph. He sipped his drink.

Suddenly, she turned to him and asked him straight out, "Did you ever touch Pet, or ask her to have sex with you, Ralph?"

"No."

The subject was never brought up again.

CHAPTER ELEVEN

Four months after giving birth to Christopher Lee, I was back in school, trying hard to catch up. It was a strain trying to get things under control, but I was happy to be away from June and Ralph, and my teachers were very helpful. I was surprised to find that most of my teachers and classmates had accepted my absence from school without question. One of my teachers, Mrs. Eugene, had called June to find out where I was, and June had told her that I'd had an accident and was in the hospital with a broken toe. It was a lame excuse, but the school accepted it. A few of my classmates even sent me cards with pictures of toes, to help me feel better about my accident. I couldn't help but smile when I looked at those cards.

Mrs. Eugene was my creative writing teacher. She was always very open and direct with me. One day, she asked me to stay after class. She told me there was an important matter that she needed to discuss with me.

"Vanessa," she said, when the others had left, "I just had to let you know that you will be cheating the world of an extraordinary talent if you do not keep up with your writing."

I was so surprised that at first I didn't understand what she was talking about.

"You should take this very seriously. You're great. You have talent."

She asked me to be her teacher's helper. I stayed after school and helped her grade papers and prepare for the next day's lessons.

On a morning in May, 1983, almost four months after Christopher Lee's birth, Mrs. Eugene told me to take my books and report to the Guidance office, adding, "Mrs. Sheppard will meet you near the stairs." I knew something was wrong. As I walked toward the stairs, I wanted to run away. But I went where I'd been told.

Mrs. Sheppard was the school social worker. She was a Black woman with a cheerful personality, always willing to talk. A few months earlier, I had gone into her office to discuss the possibility of my moving out on my own. Mrs. Sheppard had tried to talk me into staying at home and finishing high school. I had tried to explain to her why it was so important for me to leave my mother's house. I couldn't remember exactly what I'd said, but I had a feeling that my being called to her office had something to do with our last conversation.

Mrs. Sheppard had a serious look on her face. When I reached her, she put her arms around me. I could see sadness in her eyes and was afraid to ask what was wrong. She led me into her office, where I was greeted by two police officers and another Black woman.

"These officers would like to ask you a few questions about home, Vanessa," said Mrs. Sheppard.

I pulled myself away from her.

"What's this about?" I asked, not really wanting an answer.

"Vanessa, as a social worker, it's my duty to report all suspected cases of child abuse," Mrs. Sheppard replied. "I had to contact the Children's Aid Society about what we talked about. They're here to help you, but you need to tell them what you told me about your stepfather and your mother."

She gave me another hug and left me in the office with the three strangers.

The Black woman introduced herself first. Her name was Theresa Jones and she was the supervisor at the Children's Aid Office. Theresa did most of the talking. I guessed that she was supposed to make me feel more at ease, seeing as we both had the same Black heritage. It wasn't working.

"Vanessa, we'll be going to the Children's Aid office, where these officers will take a statement from you," Theresa said. "You don't have to be afraid. We're here because Mrs. Sheppard thinks you need help. We need to know what is going on at home."

I got the impression that it had already been decided that I would go to the CAS office. I had no choice in the matter.

At the door, the two officers took hold of my arms — one on either side. They led me out to a police car parked outside the front doors of the school. A few students were standing by the front door, and I couldn't help noticing their stares as I was escorted past them by the two officers, with Theresa trailing behind us. I bowed my head, trying to block out the humiliation I was feeling. I closed my eyes and hoped that when I opened them I wouldn't be with these strangers. No such luck. When I opened my eyes, I was being put into the back seat of the police cruiser.

I turned my head to see who was standing at the front doors looking at me. There were at least fourteen students. I knew that this incident would be the talk of the school for a long time to come.

I said nothing during the ride to the Children's Aid office. I closed my eyes again and refused to believe that Mrs. Sheppard had done this to me. I had trusted her, after I'd promised myself that I wouldn't trust any adults, and she had betrayed me, just like Ralph and June, Paula and Dr. Stevenson. She had called the police on me, and now I was in trouble.

I despised being in Canada. I had nothing here but heartache. I didn't know a lot of people, and the people I did know had a way of messing me up. Back in Trinidad, I may not have had fast food and telephones, but at least my life was simple there, and I'd had some good times.

When we got to the Children's Aid office, Theresa left me in a small room filled with books and toys. There were two child-sized tables, four chairs, and a couch in one corner. A Boy George video was playing on a television mounted on the wall. I watched it and wondered if Boy George knew that there were so many unhappy people in the world.

Before the video ended, Theresa came back and turned off the television. I looked at her and realized that her features reminded me of one of my aunts in Trinidad. This softened me a bit towards her. Slowly, she walked over and sat down on the couch beside me. She put her arms around me and looked into my eyes. I saw at once that she didn't want to hurt me. I longed to be able to trust her. I needed to tell someone how frightened I was.

"Vanessa, your mother is here in another room, and I'm afraid that she's denying everything you told Mrs. Sheppard. She claims that you're a trouble-maker and that you're making things up in order to break up her marriage. She claims that you've never liked your stepfather and that you're just saying that he's having sex with you so she'll leave him."

Tears flooded down my cheeks. I felt as if June had just punched me in the stomach. How could she tell such lies to strangers? Even if it was hard for her to believe at first, I didn't understand why she was still denying what was so obvious. I knew that she knew. I'd known she knew since the night she heard him. I'd been home from the hospital for almost a month. Ralph came into my room while I was sleeping and began taking off my panties. I woke up and started to struggle. "Leave me alone!" I yelled.

"Keep your ass quiet," he responded, putting his hand over my mouth and nose. I couldn't get any air, and I felt myself blacking out. Finally, I got one of my hands free. I struck out at him, temporarily releasing his grip on my face.

"I'll fucking kill you!" I screamed.

Ralph stood up. "You're not worth it." He left the room, slamming the door behind him. I could hear his footsteps as he walked back to my mother's bed.

June made no mention of this incident the next day. She never slept soundly, so I knew she couldn't have slept through my swearing and screaming. I knew then that she knew what her husband was up to and that she'd chosen to do nothing.

Sitting there in the Children's Aid office with a strange Black woman trying to comfort me, I felt that June should have been there in her place.

Once Theresa had finished telling me where I stood with my mother, the two officers who had taken me from school came into the room. The male officer asked me a few questions. He confirmed my address and age, and asked me if I knew the difference between the truth and lies. I was offended by his questions, and my guard went up. I wasn't going to sit there and let them call me a liar the way June was doing.

The male officer left, and the female officer sat down next to Theresa. "Why don't you tell me when your stepfather started making sexual advances towards you, Vanessa?" she said.

"One year ago," I answered, careful not to say anything that could get me into more trouble.

"What did your stepfather say?"

I hesitated. I tried to remember what I had told Mrs. Sheppard. If I was going to get into trouble, I wanted it to be only for the things they already knew. I wasn't going to give them anything else to hold against me.

"He said he wanted to teach me about how to please a man and how to kiss properly. We don't talk a lot."

"Did you ever tell anyone about what your stepfather was doing to you?"

"My mother and three of my friends at school."

They took the names of the friends I'd told, and finished the questioning. No one mentioned the baby, and I didn't either. I didn't want them to drag Christopher into this mess.

The male officer returned and told me my friend Trish was being questioned.

The three adults all seemed to be talking to me at once. I felt as if I was caught in a whirlwind of questions.

"When will I be going home?"

I looked at the officers, but they excused themselves and left the room. Theresa sat beside me again.

"You'll be going to an emergency foster home, Vanessa," she told me. "It will only be for a little while — until we're able to make sure that you won't be hurt any more when you return home."

Theresa took me to an old house on Oakwood Avenue. I'd never been in that part of Toronto before, and the unfamiliar surroundings made me nervous.

"You'll only be here for a short while," she reassured me again.

It was already dark outside when we got to the house. We were greeted by a middle-aged Black woman with a wide smile. She was obviously expecting us. A young Black girl appeared.

"Hi," she said. "I'm Amanda."

She took my school bag and invited me to follow her upstairs. As I followed her, I noticed five elderly people sitting at a table in a downstairs room, having dinner. I looked up at Amanda questioningly.

"You're going to be staying upstairs," she explained. "They live down here. They don't bother anyone."

Amanda looked only a few years older than me. I wondered what she'd done to end up in a place like this.

"You have nothing to be worried about," Amanda added. "Four more kids live upstairs, so you'll have lots of people to play with."

Walking up the dark staircase, I was afraid to ask questions.

Theresa was still downstairs, talking to the older woman. I could hear bits and pieces of the conversation and gathered that Theresa was explaining my situation to the woman.

Amanda took me into a small room off the hallway. "This'll be your room."

There were two single beds and an old lamp sitting on the nightstand between them. The walls were painted a very dark blue, and grey curtains covered a small window. I looked at Amanda, wishing she could tell me this was all a big mistake. Her big brown eyes looked worried, and I felt guilty for troubling her.

I was shaking and I started to cry again. I wanted to die. I couldn't understand how June could have allowed things to go so far that I'd ended up living with strangers.

"Why don't you make yourself comfortable?" she said. "I'm going to get things ready for you."

I looked around the room and tried desperately not to feel so bad. The kids in the other room were laughing at something on television. I lay down on the bed, hugging my knees and rocking.

I was so overcome by fear and anger that I didn't notice Theresa come into the room. She sat down on the bed beside me and started to stroke my hair. I cried harder and begged her to take me home.

"You'll only be here for a little while, Vanessa," she consoled me. "I'll be by sometime tomorrow to take you shopping for some clothes. You won't be going to school for a couple of days. We just need some time to figure out what we're going to do."

"I don't want to stay here," I wailed.

"It's not so bad. When you get to know everyone you'll feel a lot better."

"I don't *want* to get to know anyone."

"I know that things are hard for you to understand right now. It'll get better soon."

"Why did you bring me here?"

"We didn't have a choice, Vanessa. If your stepfather is abusing you at home, which I believe he is, then it's not safe for you to be there. The Children's Aid is here to protect children from being hurt." Theresa paused. "Do you understand?"

"I don't know."

I really wanted to believe what she was saying. I wanted to believe that she was going to make Ralph stop having sex with me. I wanted her to make June see that Ralph was wrong. I still didn't want to be there, but I wanted Theresa to help me.

"I believe you, Vanessa. I know how hard it must be for you, knowing that your mother doesn't believe you. Maybe if you're not home for a while, she'll have some time to sort out her own feelings. This way you'll at least have some outside support when you do go back home."

"Why doesn't she just believe me and make him stop?"

"A lot of mothers find it hard to deal with the fact that their spouses are actually doing this to their daughters. Some mothers do believe it, but they convince themselves it can't really be happening. A lot of these women need counselling before they can accept the truth."

"So why am I being punished for what my stepfather did?"

"You're not being punished, Vanessa," she assured me. "You were taken into care because we believe that you're in need of protection. We're concerned for your safety. We believe that what you said happened did happen. We only have your best interests in mind."

"What are you going to do with me?"

"First, we're going to try to figure out what your needs are. Then we're going to try to meet those needs ... You'll be assigned a social worker who will answer all your questions. In the meantime, it's important that you try to get comfortable and relax. No one here is going to hurt you."

Theresa left, and I lay back down on the bed, thinking about what she'd told me.

Amanda returned and told me, "You need to get washed up for snack."

I didn't understand at first. The television was turned off, and the other children were already seated at the table. Amanda walked me to the washroom so I could wash up, then guided me to the dining room, where the table was laid out with lots of different kinds of fruit. I was seated next to a girl who looked to be about fourteen years old.

"I'm Tammy," she said. "You're in my room."

"I'm Vanessa."

"I know. You're fifteen. What are you in for?"

"That ain't none of your business," Amanda jumped in. "Why don't you just finish your snack?"

"I was just asking," Tammy protested.

"Well, you should know not to mind other people's personal business."

"This is Davey, and that's Matthew," Tammy said, pointing to two young boys sitting by themselves. "They just came in last week. And that's Clyde." She indicated an older boy. "He's pretty cool."

"What would you like to eat, Vanessa?" Amanda asked.

"Anything, thank you."

Tammy was very talkative. She was open about herself and didn't seem to be ashamed about living in a foster home. I ate an apple, then went into the TV room to watch some television.

I felt strange watching Amanda and the children. They were acting as if nothing was out of the ordinary.

At nine that night we were all told to get ready for bed. I followed Tammy into our room and sat on the bed that was to be mine.

Amanda came in with a pair of pyjamas, two pairs of white socks, two panties, and a small bag with toothpaste, soap and a toothbrush for me.

"Remember to pick up some deodorant when you go shopping tomorrow," she said.

She said goodnight and left. There were a lot of questions I wanted to ask Tammy.

"Is this your first time in care?" Tammy asked me.

"Yes."

"It's not so bad. You get used to it after a while. I've been in care since I was five. My mother was into drugs. I've never seen my father. I'm being assessed for a foster home, but I think I want to go live independent after I leave here. I'm almost sixteen, I want to move out on my own on my birthday."

"I'm going to be here until my mother sorts out some stuff," I offered. "The social worker says it'll be until they can figure out what's best for me."

"Well, I wish you luck. I was supposed to be in CAS care until my mother got some help with her drug problem. That was almost ten years ago."

"My mother just needs to work some things out."

"That's good. Would you like a cigarette?"

"I have a pack."

I had been smoking for almost four months. It was really hard at first, but now that I had the hang of it, I wanted to smoke whenever I had nothing else to do.

"Are we allowed to smoke here?" I asked, with a cigarette already in my mouth.

"No. But you can smoke outside if you get permission from your worker. I just open the window and smoke with my head outside. The door is locked," Tammy explained, leaning out the window and lighting her cigarette.

I joined her, and enjoyed the cigarette more than I usually did. I tried to forget all that had happened that day and listened to Tammy. She told me all about living in a foster home and dealing with the house parents.

I tried to fall asleep after Tammy said good night, but my mind was racing and my head had started to hurt. Two hours after the house fell silent, I was still awake. Everyone else was asleep and I could hear the sound of their breathing, and a variety of night noises. Tammy was snoring loudly. I couldn't get Ralph out of my mind. I didn't feel safe.

I got out of bed and crawled into a small closet in the corner of the room. I shut the door, curled up in the corner and started to rock back and forth. I don't remember falling asleep, but I woke suddenly in the morning when Tammy opened the closet door and started to laugh.

"Are you afraid of sleeping alone?"

"No," I lied. "I can't sleep with noise, and you were snoring really loud."

"Sorry. What are you doing today?"

"The social worker who brought me here said that she was coming to take me shopping."

"Theresa's really cool. She was my worker for a while last year. She'll make sure you get some good things."

Amanda walked by in the hall and called out to me, "Better get dressed if you plan on going shopping today!"

I felt uncomfortable taking off my pyjamas in front of Tammy. I put on the clothes I'd been wearing the day before and found that they had been washed and dried during the night.

"What do you want for breakfast?" Amanda asked, walking into the room.

"Anything," I said.

"Miss Tammy, you better get your ass off to school — if you miss another class it's Section 27 for you," said Amanda before leaving.

I looked at Tammy.

"Section 27 is a special kind of classroom where troubled kids go instead of regular school. Mostly kids from group homes and foster homes. It's kind of like a jail. They have all these group home staff there, and they follow you around wherever you go. They even follow you to the fucking *washroom*."

"Why would you have to go there?"

"Because I've been skipping a few classes. But it's not so bad. There's a lot of cool guys there. I don't give a shit, but I have to go to school today because I'm getting some grass." Tammy got dressed and left without eating breakfast. By the time I went downstairs, the other three kids had also left for school. Amanda was busy in the kitchen.

"Good morning," I said.

"Don't look like you had such a good night."

"What do you mean?"

"You didn't sleep in your bed. I went to get your clothes this morning and you were sound asleep in the closet."

I ducked my head. I'd had no idea that she knew. She saw my embarrassment and said gently, "My lips are sealed."

"I needed to be in a quiet place."

"Well, next time, let me know when you're not comfortable, and I'll try to help."

"Thank you."

For the next hour, Amanda showed me around the big old house. I saw the back of the house and learned where the list of chores was kept. I also learned more about the other people who were living in the house.

The five elderly people I'd seen the night before lived downstairs and had their own rooms. They paid the owner of the house for their room, board and care. They were taken to their doctor's appointments and had their medication brought to them each night. For the last few years, the house mother had also been taking in children for the Children's Aid Society. She had as many as six children staying there at a time, some for as little as a few hours, some for as long as six months.

The two youngest boys, Davey and Matthew, had been taken away from their mother two weeks ago after her boyfriend was arrested for physically assaulting them both.

Tammy had been telling the truth when she said that she'd been in the care of the CAS since she was five years old. She'd had a very hard life. She'd already had two abortions, and she'd been in trouble with the law. She'd spent time in detention for attempted murder. Four years earlier, when she was only eleven, she had stabbed her mother and left her for dead. It made me kind of uncomfortable to realize that I was sharing a room with someone who had tried to kill her mother. Looking at Tammy's cheerful face, I would never have guessed that she was capable of such violence.

Amanda explained that each week I could make three phone calls and go out with my friends once. I had to be in the house two and a half hours after school, and I could have guests over after I'd finished an orientation period which lasted for a month.

"Are you all right?" she asked, as I tried to digest what she'd just told me.

"I'm not going to be here for very long anyway," I said.

"I know. But it's good for you to know how things work here, just in case you have to stay for a bit longer."

The door bell rang and she went to answer it. I sat at the kitchen table, wondering how I'd get through this mess.

Theresa walked into the kitchen and gave me a hug. She looked a lot younger than I remembered. She wore an earth-coloured two-piece outfit with shorts, and matching sandals. Her chocolate-coloured skin had a healthy shine and so did her hair. She had peaceful brown eyes and wore little make-up. She'd brought me a cheese danish and a cup of coffee. She sat down next to me and started to drink her own coffee.

"I know they don't have coffee here for you kids," she said. "Amanda thinks it makes you hyper. *I* think there should be a law that everyone has to have a cup of coffee before going anywhere in the morning."

I was taken by surprise — Theresa was speaking to me as if I was an adult. She seemed happy to see me, which made me feel a bit better.

"Where do you want to go?" she asked.

"I don't know."

"Well, let me surprise you, and then I'll take you out for lunch."

"When am I going back to school?"

"I think it'll be best for you to take some time off and get yourself together before you start going to school again."

"How long will I be out of school?"

"Well, that's one of the things I'd like to talk to you about later today, Vanessa. Why don't we wait until after lunch?"

"Why do we need to go shopping?"

"Well, if you intend to go back to school anytime in the near future, you'll need clothes."

"Why can't we just get some clothes from home?"

"Your mother is very upset that your stepfather was arrested and charged with sexual exploitation yesterday. It's going to take awhile for her to calm down enough to let us go and get your things. In the meantime, you're still going to be needing clothes."

The news that Ralph had been charged came as a total shock. I wasn't happy about it, but certainly I wasn't sad. "What did my mother do when he was charged?"

"She's standing by your stepfather, and she's made it clear that she's going to be supporting him. I'm sorry she's not supporting you, Vanessa."

"Why isn't she going to help me?" I was weak with disappointment.

"She's denying that he ever touched you. She says you're a liar."

I began to tremble and cry again. Theresa put her arms around me. "It's not your fault that all this has happened, Vanessa."

"Whose fault is it then?"

"You are the victim here, Vanessa. Your stepfather deserves to be punished, not you. You have to stop blaming yourself and feeling sorry for your mother and everyone else. It's time for you to start looking out for yourself."

CHAPTER TWELVE

Almost a month after I had moved into the big old house, Amanda told me I'd be moving soon, to a group home on Browning Avenue. I was crushed. I'd spent a lot of energy getting used to this family and I really didn't want to start over again.

"You'll do just fine, Vanessa," she said.

"I don't like living with strangers."

"I know it's hard for you right now. Just try to make the best of things."

"Is it all right if I go over to the park for a while?"

"Sure. Try and be back for supper."

I went up to my room and took out my diary. Lately, it was my best friend. I got my purse and left for the park.

Since I'd been taken into the care of the Children's Aid Society, I hadn't spoken to June at all. I was feeling more and more that she was to blame for what was happening to me. And the more I heard about her denying that Ralph had abused me, the less I wanted to be around her.

At the park, I watched two young girls playing tennis and wondered what their worst nightmares were. I wondered if they had ever experienced anything close to what had happened to me. What would they think if they knew about my life? I decided that they'd probably think that I was wrong, just like everyone else did.

I walked until I found a tall tree. I lay down on the grass beneath it, closed my eyes and enjoyed the peace and quiet. The June breeze warmed my skin as it blew a few strands of my hair over my face. The smell greenery and flowers filled the air, and the new grass was like a soft carpet. I wished I could lie there forever.

I was about to write a poem in my mind about how peaceful I was feeling when I realized someone was standing over me. I was about to scream, but instead I opened my eyes and recognized the worried brown eyes that were staring at me.

"Are you all right?"

"Charles." My heart was still pounding. "I'm fine." I pulled myself to a sitting position and tried to wipe the surprise off my face.

"Where have you been hiding?"

Avoiding his eyes, I said, "I'm living right across the street."

"I don't live too far myself. Would you like to visit?"

"No. I have to get going."

"You take care of yourself and try to get better soon."

He turned to go, then changed his mind and turned back to me.

"Look, Vanessa." He took my hand. "No one's gonna look out for you but you. I know something must be wrong for your mother to say that I was responsible for making you pregnant." He sounded more like his usual self now. He gazed into my eyes.

"I don't know what's up," he went on, "but I don't believe that you would blame me for something I had nothing to do with. I was surprised, but not mad."

"I'm sorry for what my mother did," I said, hanging my head and closing my eyes. "She had no right to drag you into this."

"Is everything all right with the baby?"

I raised my head, but didn't open my eyes. "He's dead." Then I opened my eyes, just in time to see the shock on Charles's face.

"Do you ever visit the grave?"

"My mother took care of the burial. She hasn't told me where he's buried. I only saw him for a few minutes."

"Don't you want to know?"

"More than anything else in the world. But my mother doesn't want to talk about it. She still blames me for messing up her life."

"You're very strong."

"No, I'm not. I just pretend because I don't know what else to do."

"I hope that things work out for you, Ness." He had often called me that when we were in Cadets. "I wish you had told me you had a boyfriend," he added, sounding hurt.

I could have hit him for even suggesting that I might have been having sex with someone without telling him. "I never had a boyfriend," I blurted out. "I was raped!" I started to cry.

Charles, the one guy who had always listened to me without wanting anything in return, reached over and hugged me. I didn't try to pull away. It was nice to be cared for by another human being.

We talked for a little longer. A lot of 'if onlys' came into the conversation.

"If you knew, what would you have done?" I asked him.

"I really can't say. I think you've handled everything really well."

Charles and I said goodbye and I promised to keep in touch. I picked up my things and headed back to the foster home.

I hadn't talked about Christopher since that encounter with my stepfather. Talking with Charles about the baby brought back a lot of emotions I had been trying to keep under control. I couldn't help but wonder whether he died in pain. I wondered if he was alone or if someone was there to hold his hand.

I could still feel his small fingers and toes.

I still had the urge to hold him in my arms.

I wanted to put flowers on his grave.

I hadn't told anyone how I felt. No one would understand why it was so important for me to know what had really happened to Christopher.

Two days after I saw Charles, I moved to a group home on Browning Avenue. It was very different from the foster home where I'd spent the past month.

At this house, there were different people on staff, and they worked eight and twelve-hour shifts. The kids were called "residents" — it was clear that this was not a home. There were lots of rules. I couldn't go outside without getting permission from a staff member. Every day we had to sit in the living room for "quiet time." All the residents got their homework or something to read or write and sat quietly for an hour. I used the time to bury my head in a book, not wanting to be drawn into the whispered conversations that took place between the others. We could make phone calls only during specified hours and each call had to be over in ten minutes. Bedtime was at nine-thirty, and all lights had to be turned out by ten. This made me uptight, as I usually wrote in my diary at night. At the foster home, I'd been allowed to stay up as long as I wanted and write as much as I needed.

There were male and female residents. I'd counted eight different staff members, including two students who worked at the group home as part of their college programs. The person who said goodnight to me was usually not the person who woke me up in the morning. Different activities were planned for the residents almost every day. Sometimes we had to stay in the house and do woodwork in the basement.

Every time the phone rang, I held my breath, hoping it was Elaine calling to tell me that my mother had finally told the truth about what my stepfather had done and that I could go back home.

I'd no news about what was happening to Ralph. Since the day Theresa told me he'd been arrested, I hadn't heard anything.

Shortly after I moved into the group home, my new social worker, Elaine Trout, took me to a hearing at a family court on Jarvis Street. It was the first time I had seen June since I was taken away. As she sat in the court and listened to the judge give the Children's Aid Society wardship of me, she said nothing. She didn't even look at me.

After the court hearing, I felt numb as Elaine drove me back to the group home. My eyes ached from crying.

"You'll be starting with a sexual abuse group for teen-age girls next week," Elaine informed me. "I'll pick you up next Thursday."

I faintly remembered hearing her mention this to Anne-Marie Soame, my new primary worker at the group home.

"There you are," Anne-Marie said, walking up behind me. "What do you say we spend some time together?"

I had found a comfortable spot on the front porch, and I pressed my face deeper into my hands when I heard Anne-Marie's voice.

I had met Anne-Marie once before, the day after I got placed in the new home. I still couldn't remember everyone's name, but I recognized Anne-Marie because of her hair. It reached her waist and looked like a waterfall when it was loose. Anne-Marie had been very polite when she introduced herself to me. Even though I knew I had to keep my guard up around these strangers, I couldn't help but like this one. She had promised that when she was back on shift she would spend some one-on-one time with me. I didn't know what she meant, but it worried me. I didn't want to be put through another questioning session or be forced to talk about Ralph.

Now, Anne-Marie asked me if I'd like to go for a walk. I let my hands fall from my face, and looked up at her. I admired the way her hair glowed in the sun. She wore almost no make-up, but still she managed to shine like a pretty doll. She was smiling at me and I couldn't resist smiling back. It was a small smile, but it was still a smile.

There was silent concern in her soft, deep eyes. Why didn't my mother ever look at me like that? I was getting that feeling in my body again, the aching feeling. I started to shake.

"It's all right to cry, Vanessa." Anne-Marie said, sitting next to me. She reached over and put her arms around me. I wanted to get lost in them. It felt safe. I let her comfort me.

CHAPTER THIRTEEN

I was glad to see Elaine when she picked me up the following Thursday. I still hadn't made any friends at the group home. After supper, the night before, I'd stolen a knife from the kitchen while doing the dishes.

I wasn't too worried about the female staff at the group home. Most of them were quite friendly and easy to get along with. But anytime I found myself alone with any of the men — especially if they spoke to me — my heartbeat would quicken, and I would feel like I was going to suffocate.

After our encounter on the porch, Anne-Marie was off for almost four days, and when she came back she was on the midnight shift. We hadn't discussed my outburst, but I just knew that she understood.

"How's everything going?" Elaine asked.

I was almost ecstatic just to be away from the group home.

"I don't know."

"The staff called and gave me an update. I hear you're still quite withdrawn. Are you feeling all right?"

"Same as always."

"You know the staff is there for you to talk to if you need anything. And you can always call me if you really need to talk to me."

"Thanks."

"Vanessa," she said, "I want you to know that I believe you, and I'll do whatever I can to help you get through this."

"Thank you," I repeated.

I wished I could tell Elaine that it had nothing to do with her, that I couldn't talk to anyone or make friends while I had my own problems. The situation with my stepfather and my mother was not what was bothering me most at that point. It was the issue nobody ever brought up: my baby. Six months had passed since I'd given birth, and I still didn't know where he was. I felt like I couldn't do anything until I found out where he was and said goodbye.

"Here we are," Elaine said. I hadn't said another word to her. "Are you sure that you're all right?"

"Yes."

"This group will help you deal with what your dad did to you."

I wanted to correct her. Ralph was not my father. He was my stepfather; it was so important to me that I remember that.

"I'll pick you up after the session. Hurry up, or you'll be late."

As I walked into the room where the meeting was taking place, a babble of voices rose to meet me. People were standing around in small groups, talking. I slowly made my way to the back of the room, where an empty chair sat away from the traffic. There were six girls, I figured they were here for the same reason as myself. There were some mothers and some other adults whom I assumed were social workers.

Absorbed in my own thoughts, I didn't notice at first when the room quieted down. I looked up and saw that only two adults were left in the room, and that the other girls had seated themselves in a semi-circle. I felt stupid sitting in the back of the room, with all eyes focused on me.

"We've got someone new with us today," one of the two women announced. She turned to me. "Would you like to introduce yourself?"

I got up from the chair and knocked it over by accident.

"Why don't you come and join us?" asked the other woman. "You don't have to say anything if you don't feel comfortable."

I went over to where they had seated themselves, and one of the girls passed me a mat to sit on.

"You're Vanessa, right?" the first woman asked.

I bobbed my head up and down in response.

"I'm Maggie. That's Brenda." She pointed to the other woman.

I looked over at Brenda and forced a smile. All the girls were looking at me.

"I'm sorry," I said, feeling awkward.

Each girl introduced herself, and I began to feel a bit more comfortable. As it turned out, I'd only missed one session. Maggie and Brenda, the group leaders, explained to me the reasons for the group and how it worked.

"Why don't we start by talking about how we're feeling today?" suggested Maggie. "Try to reach inside and pull out your feelings."

Brenda looked around. "Who'd like to start?"

"I'm still angry at my uncle," Annie said.

Annie was a Native girl. She was only twelve years old but she wore a lot of make-up, so she looked older. She had a perm in her hair, making it extra curly.

"It's like he did nothing wrong," she said. "Here I am, and he's eating barbecue at my parents' house. They act like nothing even happened."

"How do you feel about your parents' attitude towards him?" asked Maggie.

"I hate both of them. I hate them and I wish they were both dead!"

Another girl, Sandy, said, "My mother still does my brother's laundry, cooks his breakfast and even cleans his room. She wouldn't even let me come home for weekend visits. She says it would upset Bobby ... Everything is Bobby — Bobby is going to play professional hockey, Bobby has a part-time job, Bobby needs this, Bobby needs that. She never thinks about what I need."

"At Christmas she called my foster home and cancelled my visit. She said there was going to be lots of family at the house, and she wouldn't be able to keep an eye on me, it was going to cause too many problems to have me around. Why is it that after my brother forced me to have sex with him, I'm getting punished for what he did? As far as they're concerned, I'm causing embarrassment to the whole family." Sandy started to cry. "What about Sandy?" she shouted. "What about my feelings? Why am I the one who gets punished?"

"It's not your fault, Sandy." Brenda put her arms around the crying girl.

Then Sarah spoke up. "My mother didn't know what was going on with me and my father until three months ago, when she walked in on us having sex."

Sarah was also only twelve years old. She was petite and had short blonde hair. As she spoke, she rested her head on the shoulder of the girl next to her.

"My father has been performing oral sex on me for as long as I can remember. He always started right after I had my bath. When my mother was at work, he'd fill the bathtub and call me to have a bath with him. I feel really guilty because most of the time when he put his mouth on my privates it felt good. It kind of felt like I was melting. He always said that I tasted so good. Sometimes he would make me go to his room and he would put honey on my crotch and push my legs wide open. It didn't hurt. He'd lick off all the honey and then put some on his penis and make me lick it off. At first it used to choke me because when he got hard in my mouth I couldn't breathe."

"The worst was when he'd make me swallow his sperm. He kept telling me how good it tasted. It didn't taste good at all, it used to make me gag. Then after a few years, he put his penis in me. It hurt so much. It took a few times for him to put it all in. Then after a while it didn't hurt so much, just a little when he didn't put enough vaseline. But after he finished he always kissed my privates and licked them to make me feel better. He was going to teach me how to have an orgasm." Sarah's eyes watered, and she stared into space.

"He said that it wasn't wrong to feel good. When he had oral sex with me it did feel good, so I thought that nothing was wrong. And he always bought me whatever I wanted. Even when Mom said no, I always ended up getting it. I feel that if I didn't like the feelings, maybe he wouldn't have done it for so long. In a way it's my fault."

All eyes were on Sarah. No one moved, and I could almost hear my heart beat. I couldn't breathe. I was afraid to even blink.

Finally Maggie broke the silence.

"First of all, Sarah, you are not responsible for what your father did. He started to perform oral sex on you when you were only three years old. You didn't have a choice.

"It is a perfectly normal thing to feel a good physical sensation when someone is performing oral sex on you. It has nothing to do with you wanting it. There's nothing wrong with enjoying the experience when you're old enough to make that decision and when it's with someone you want to experience it with. Your body responds to certain kinds of stimulation, whether you want it to or not. When children are exposed to sexual stimulation at such a young age, they are powerless to do anything to control their response to it."

Then Brenda spoke, looking at each of us in turn. "A lot of adults have problems controlling their sexual emotions. A child can't be expected to be able to make sense of adult feelings."

"For a while I didn't know it was wrong, but when he started making me lie to my mother about what we were doing all day, I knew something wasn't right," said Sarah. "I still love him so much. I can't hate him. That's the only bad thing he ever did to me. He's good in every other way."

"There's nothing wrong with loving your father. That's normal," said Maggie. "But it doesn't mean that you have to love the things he did. He assaulted you and that was wrong. No one has the right to your body unless you give them the okay."

I was amazed. I was still so ashamed of what had happened to me that I couldn't even bring myself to admit openly that it had happened, and here were all these other girls, just spilling their secrets. I wanted to kill all the men who had hurt them.

I was shocked to find out that many of these girls' mothers didn't believe them either. All this time, I had thought that June was the only one. Why wouldn't these mothers listen to their daughters?

Brenda put her hands on my shoulders. "Vanessa, are you all right?"

"Yes ... I'm just a bit thirsty."

"Well, we're finished for today. Hope you'll join us again next week." She indicated a table set up in a corner of the room. "You can help yourself to a snack over there. Why don't you get to know some of the other girls?"

I wandered through the room, trying not to make eye contact with any of the girls. I didn't want anyone to see my tear-stained face.

After what seemed like forever, Elaine picked me up. I felt worse than when she had dropped me off. I was so angry I wanted to hurt myself, and I wanted to hurt my stepfather for making me feel like that.

Elaine took me out for ice cream before returning me to the home. I didn't say a word to her until she dropped me off. Then I told her that I wasn't going back there.

"Why don't we talk about it later? Maybe you need some time to think it over."

I told the staff that I wasn't feeling well, and went up to my room to rest. I got into bed feeling so dirty, like I had just been raped. I didn't want to go back to that group. I didn't want to talk about what Ralph had done to me. I couldn't let anyone else find out.

CHAPTER FOURTEEN

In August, I was taken to a psychiatrist, an older man, for an assessment. He asked a lot of questions that meant absolutely nothing to me, then he made me draw some pictures and put some puzzles together.

"How do you feel about your mother and your stepfather?" he asked.

"I don't know," I answered honestly.

I was glad when the session was over.

I began to wonder about what it would be like to be dead and not have to deal with anyone. How would it feel to be up in the clouds, free from all the confusion that I was feeling? The more I thought about it, the more pleasant it seemed. I thought about dying more and more. Sometimes it was all I could think about. I started to write down my thoughts and feelings about death, and once I did, things didn't seem all that bad.

On September 13, 1983, I had to go to court again. I didn't understand most of it, but then I wasn't paying much attention. I looked around and realized that June wasn't in court this time. I was made a Crown Ward. After the court session, Elaine explained that the Children's Aid Society was now my legal guardian, and would be responsible for my well-being until I reached the age of majority. I would only have access to my mother (at her convenience), my brothers, and my grandmother. I laughed inside: my mother didn't speak to me any more, my brothers didn't know where I was (and even if they did, Jerome was the only one who would have wanted to see me), and I hadn't been able to get in touch with my grandmother for more than two years.

Simply put, I was now disowned.

The next day, a lawyer was appointed to advise me and to work as my advocate. Things were just flying past me.

Later that day, Anne-Marie came up to my room to see me. She asked, "How are you dealing with what happened with your stepfather?"

I didn't know what she was talking about, so I just looked at her.

"You know that the Crown attorney and the police have decided to drop the charges against your stepfather, don't you?"

I shook my head.

"Isn't that what you met with them about last week?" she asked.

"They just asked me how I was holding up, and told me that going to court was kind of scary."

"They say that you all decided that it was the best thing to do under the circumstances. Don't you remember talking with them about withdrawing the charges?"

"No ... I'm having a hard time keeping track of everything that's going on, but I would remember something that important."

"The Children's Aid Society seems to agree that it's best if you don't have to go to court," said Anne-Marie. "Your mother is very supportive of your stepfather, and things might have gotten dirty."

Lately, I just agreed with whatever the Children's Aid told me. I signed all the forms, I did what I was supposed to do. All the while, I kept thinking about how nice it would be to die and get away from it all.

One day, I walked into my room in the group home to find one of the other girls there. I saw her put my diary back in my dresser.

"What are you doing in my things?" I asked.

"I'm not in your things. I was just looking for my brush."

"Please don't touch my things."

"Fuck yourself!" she said, and left.

The next day, I went to her room and took some of her clothes and a pair of her shoes. With the stolen knife that I'd hidden in my pillow, I cut two of her dresses to shreds. I stuck the rest of the clothes and the shoes in my closet. Every time I saw her with my diary or anything else that was mine, I was going to cut up something of hers.

The next evening, Anne-Marie called me into the office.

"Vanessa, did you steal anything from anyone's room?"

"No."

"Do you have anything that belongs to another resident?"

"No."

"You know that I'll have to do a room search, don't you?"

"Yes."

"Are you sure there's nothing in your room that I should know about?"

Tears rolled down my cheeks, but I kept silent. The other girl started it by taking my diary. My diary was a lot more important than some clothes.

When the clothes and shoes were found in my room, my allowance of seven dollars was taken away to replace the clothes I'd destroyed, but I didn't care. Whenever a resident did something to me, I stole something of his or hers, and more often than not, I felt better after I destroyed it. Being able to take their things and not get caught, at least not right away, made me feel good. But I always got caught eventually, though I never once admitted to taking anything. After a while, the staff would automatically come to me when something went missing. The residents prayed that I wouldn't get hold of their things, as they knew what would happen if I did. Anne-Marie tried to talk to me about what I was doing, but I tuned her out and continued to take knives from the kitchen whenever I could. Nothing mattered anymore. No one cared about me, so why should I care about them?

I walked around in another world — my world. I was the boss of my own life. Sometimes I'd leave school, walk over to the cemetery and look at all the headstones. I closed my eyes and tried to *feel* whether my baby was buried there. I was thinking about him more and more. I started to look around other cemeteries in the area. I still felt like I couldn't get on with my life till I found out where he was. I had to find him.

CHAPTER FIFTEEN

L ater that summer, I was sent to the Clarke Institute of Psychiatry for another assessment. This one was part of a program especially for Black kids. It was supposed to make me feel more at home, but the other five youths in the program were nothing to feel homey about. I wondered whether the Institute had searched the whole of Toronto to find the five most violent and badly-behaved Black kids.

Every time Children's Aid arranged to get me the help it thought I needed, I came out a lot more confused and frustrated than ever. But they just seemed to think that the more help I received, the more I needed. I refused to go back to the Clarke Institute.

"For one thing," I explained to Elaine, "those kids need of a lot more help than I do."

"But the program is set up for kids like you," she said, trying to control her frustration.

"You mean for Blacks like me?"

"Well, if that's how you want to see it." She sighed. "All the same, I think it would be good for you to at least think about it before you make any rash decisions."

"Look," I said quietly, "I don't need to be around a bunch of whacks to realize that I'm Black. No one else in that stupid group has been raped. No one has lost a baby. No one has been forced out of their own home, lost their mother or brothers ... Being Black isn't a sickness. I don't need to go to treatment for it. I don't have cancer. All I want is to find my baby and be left alone."

At the home that night, I finished packing. I would be moving again the following week. The staff at Browning had done their jobs. They had kept a daily record of all of my outbursts and mood swings. Together with the Children's Aid Society, they had decided I was going to live in a parent-run group home. I was sick and tired of moving, getting used to strangers, then moving again and more strangers.

Just before I left Browning, my brother Jerome sneaked out to visit me without my mother or stepfather knowing. I was very happy to see him. But after just a few months of living apart, things felt different. We weren't best friends anymore. We tried, but our conversation was strained. We finally settled on not saying much.

"You miss your brother, don't you?" said Anne-Marie, after Jerome had left.

"Sometimes."

"It must be really hard getting used to everything."

"I'm just tired of all the shit. If my stepfather would just tell the truth, I wouldn't be stuck dealing with all this."

"Unfortunately it doesn't look like that's going to happen, Vanessa. You'll have to manage by yourself for a little while. Hopefully, things between you and your mother will get better soon."

"I don't even know if I care any more."

"You just have to take things one day at a time."

I had learned to like Anne-Marie, just as I had Amanda. I didn't trust her enough to tell her my secrets, but that had more to do with her being a staff member and an adult than with Anne-Marie herself.

"Will you miss me a little bit?" I asked her.

"Of course," she promised, hugging me goodbye.

I moved into the Storey Group Home in late September, 1983. There were five other kids living there: four boys, and a girl named Lydia. The group home father, Leo, never forgot to remind me that he was the boss, and his wife, Nicky, wasn't much better as far as I could see. I couldn't go out after school, which meant that I hardly ever saw Trish. We *were* allowed to smoke, but only every half hour out on the back porch. I was smoking a lot of cigarettes.

I got a new social worker, Laura. She seemed nice enough. We met a few times, but mostly we spent a lot of time on the phone, as I had an awful lot of complaining to do about my new home.

The group home and the Children's Aid were forever planning things for me to do. I always refused to participate.

It was eight months since I had given birth to Christopher, and I wanted to find him as badly as ever. I was crying all the time. I stopped paying attention to my schoolwork. Once in a while, I wondered what my life would have been like if I hadn't told Mrs. Sheppard what my stepfather was doing.

It was the final meeting of my sexual abuse support group. I felt strange. I was glad that I wouldn't have to listen to any more sad and disturbing stories, but at the same time I knew that I would miss everyone. All of us, including the group leaders, were fighting the same war.

The meeting went on as usual. Sarah was talking, then Maggie was telling her something. Then all of a sudden, in the middle of the meeting, I felt a strong wave of anger flooding over me, through my body and into my clenched fists. I was vaguely aware of my fists hitting the floor. I was angry at all the men in the world. I hated them all. I hated how they were making me feel. I wanted to scream.

I *was* screaming.

I tried to focus on what Brenda was saying to me. I could feel arms around my shoulders. Lots of arms.

"Why are we always the ones who get hurt?" someone asked.

Their faces surrounded me. So many sad faces. So many tears. I could feel myself being rocked back and forth. I began to calm down. They were all here.

"It's all right to cry, Vanessa," said Maggie comfortingly. "This is the first time that you've allowed yourself to open up. It's not fair, I know."

As I looked around the room, I saw all those eyes focused on me, not judging or condemning. Understanding eyes.

After that session, my emotional state changed drastically. A door opened that had been jammed shut for almost a year. It was like living with another person. Waves of emotion washed over me, over and over again. My crying episodes became a real problem. I had to be careful. Too many people had caught me crying already.

My anger now went beyond my parents, beyond men. It became focused on God. Why was God turning His back on me? I wondered if He blamed me too. Maybe He was only answering June's prayers. Why didn't He try to help me? I could no longer trust Him. He hadn't been around for me for a long time.

CHAPTER SIXTEEN

I was becoming obsessed with the supernatural. I felt sure that when I found out where my baby was buried, his spirit would see me and hear me. I wondered if my mother ever visited the grave. Could *she* communicate with Christopher? When I was in labour and she locked me up in my bedroom for days, had she known that if the baby was in distress long enough, it would not survive?

One day in the fall, I was sitting on a bench in a cemetery I often visited when I saw two workers lowering a small box into an open grave. I felt faint for a moment, realizing that they were about to bury a little baby without its mother.

I got up and hurried over. It didn't look like a real grave. It was so small.

The two men looked up at me as I stood there with tears in my eyes. The box the baby was in was so plain. It looked so simple, so cold. Closing my eyes, I pictured my own son being put into the cold earth without anyone there to say goodbye to him.

Deep in my mind, I could hear my grandmother's voice: "It's no use wasting your tears on the dead. They're already dead and can't feel a thing. Jesus said, 'let the dead bury the dead.'" I didn't want to believe her. It wasn't right for a baby to be buried without even a prayer.

"Are you related?" one of the men asked, puzzled.

"No ... I was just wondering why there's no one here to see it buried."

"This is just a common burial. The government is paying, and I reckon they can't come to every burial they pay for."

"I was just thinking about my baby."

"Your baby?" The man looked at me more closely. "You look a bit young to have a baby. Is he buried here?"

"I don't know where he's buried. He might be here ... I named him Christopher. I'm not sure if that's still his name. He died when I was still in the hospital. I wasn't invited to his funeral. I don't even know if he *had* a funeral." With that, I turned abruptly and went back to my bench.

When the men left, I returned to the place where they'd been working. I stood at the side of the small grave and asked the little baby to tell my son that I would find him someday.

"Tell him that I'm going to be with him soon," I added.

I left the cemetery feeling as if I had finally accomplished something.

For Christmas of 1983, I was allowed to visit my family in Trinidad. Making the arrangements was a bit complicated, but finally I was on the plane. For the first time in three years, I was going to see my grandmother.

Upon leaving the baggage checkout, I spotted her almost immediately. She looked a lot older than I remembered and she had a walking stick. She was smiling, trying to focus her eyes on me. With a shock, I finally realized why she had wanted me to go away. My God ... she was going blind.

"Pet, Pet," she cooed, stroking my hair as I flew into her arms. I started to cry. There was so much I wanted to tell her: What Ralph had done to me. What my mother had done. My baby.

"Doh talk," she whispered in my ear. "You jes relax. We go talk later."

We returned to my old home. It was so good seeing everyone. Exhausted after all the excitement, I went to bed early. I curled up next to my grandmother and slept like a baby.

The next day, Grams and I were picking flowers for her church when she brought the subject up.

"Nobody have to know about yuh secrets," she said. "People wouldn't understand. They go jes use it against you. Yuh must keep it to yuhself." She took my face in her hand. "Yuh must try to make peace with your mother. Even though she make mistakes, she is still yuh mother. De only one you have."

"But she hate me. She make dem take me away and put me in dem group homes. She doh care."

In the same calm, gentle voice, Grams answered, "But she is still yuh mother. I not going to be around forever. You must make a life for yuhself in Canada. If yuh stay here, you wouldn't have a chance. At least in Canada yuh go have a chance at a better life."

"You doh want me?"

"Of course ah want you. You is mih Pet. But ah want yuh to have a good life too."

That was the first and the last time we discussed it. In January I flew back to Canada. I was picked up from the airport by the group home parents. Things were back to normal.

CHAPTER SEVENTEEN

A year had gone by since Christopher's birth, and I was having nightmares about him again. In some of my dreams, he would be happy and laughing. He would be in heaven, being taken care of by the angels. But more often, I saw my baby in the hospital, crying, with no one there to pick him up. I saw his eyes fixed on mine. I felt his tiny fingers in my hand, and his smooth skin. Then I saw my mother and the nurses taking him away, as he cried and gasped for air. I would wake in hysterics. Jumping out of bed, still half-asleep, I would pretend that I was holding Christopher in my arms, comforting him. I would sing to him and beg him not to cry. I'd wipe away his tears, and play with the little curls on top of his head.

Then I would realize that he wasn't really in my arms. He had never been in my arms. I would remember that he was dead, and I still didn't know where he was buried. So I'd start to rock again. And I'd try to think of him in that nice safe place, asleep and smiling. In another world, where people were nice and didn't tell so many lies.

One night, after one of these nightmares, I had to get out of the group home. I was mad at everything and everyone. I let myself out through the back door and, without thinking about where I was going, headed for the cemetery.

The voices in my head were getting louder every night. Sometimes I felt consumed by guilt and shame. I felt dizzy a lot, and I was often incoherent when talking to people. This had to be what it felt like to be going crazy.

When I got to the cemetery, the gates were already closed. I stood outside for a few minutes, then walked over to the park across the street. The branches on the trees whispered in the chilly breeze. I strained to hear what they were saying, but I couldn't understand. I was fifteen years old, and I sat on a bench in a public park, crying like a newborn baby.

I took out my diary. Lighting a cigarette, I started to write. For almost two hours, I sat in the park and debated whether or not to walk over to June's house. She lived only a few minutes away. Many times before, I'd stood in the parking lot of her building, wondering whether she ever thought of me. Finally, feeling very tired, I returned to the group home. As I started up the stairs to the room I shared with Lydia, a voice behind me said, "Where the hell do you think you're going?"

I turned to see Leo standing in the living room, staring at me. His wife Nicky was sitting in a chair in the corner.

"To my room."

"We'd like to speak to you downstairs," he said loudly.

"I'm tired."

"You weren't tired when you left the house without permission."

I turned and continued upstairs. "I need to be by myself."

"This is the fifteenth time we've had to call the police to file an AWOL on you," he called after me. "You have five minutes to get downstairs."

I stripped off my clothes as soon as I got to my room. I put my diary on the dresser, put on my pajamas, and got into bed. Exactly five minutes later, the door opened and Leo and Nicky walked in.

Lydia jumped out of bed. "What's going on?" she asked, looking from them to me.

"Go out in the hallway, Lydia," said Nicky, looking at me.

"Why?"

"Get going!" shouted Leo.

Lydia got back into her bed. "I'm tired," she said.

"Get out of the fucking room, Lydia!"

Ignoring him, she looked at me. "What did you do, Vanessa?"

"Get the hell out of here!" Leo ordered. "Now!"

Lydia grabbed her comforter and brushed past Nicky. I heard whispers out in the hallway. The other kids were awake and waiting for the outcome.

Nicky walked over to my bed, as Leo locked the door. "Where were you?"

"I was sitting in the park."

"Do you expect us to believe that at four in the morning you were really in the park?" said Leo.

"That's exactly where I was. I needed some space. What's wrong with wanting to be alone?"

"Get up and come down to the living room."

"I don't want to go to the living room."

"If you don't go by yourself, I'll be happy to help you."

"Why don't you just leave me alone?"

"Because as long as you're living under this roof, Vanessa, you will do as we say. Do you understand?"

"We can talk about whatever you want tomorrow."

"We'll talk *now*."

"Why don't you do as you're told, Vanessa?" Nicky said. "Because I'm tired, and I don't feel like dealing with either of you right now."

"You don't really have a choice in this matter."

Rolling over to face the wall, I repeated, "I'm tired."

Leo walked up to me and grabbed my arms, hard. Nicky took hold of my hands and forced them behind my back. They lifted me to my feet and with almost no effort dragged me out of the room.

"Get back to bed," Leo snapped at the other kids as we passed them in the corridor.

My ankle twisted as they dragged me down the stairs. As we entered the living room, Nicky let go of me, but Leo tightened his grip. He shoved me to the ground and, still holding my arm, put his knee in the middle of my back. This was the second time he had restrained me like this — the first had been when I refused to hand over my cigarettes. Meanwhile, Nicky disappeared, then came back with some of my belongings in her arms. "You won't be getting any of these things back until you can straighten out your act."

Finally, Leo released me and shoved me into a chair.

"That's my diary," I said to Nicky. "You don't have the right to take away my diary."

"Just watch me." She started leafing through the pages. "Maybe whoever you were with tonight is listed in here."

"Don't," I said.

"What are you going to do?"

"I'm not joking."

Leo yanked me up from the chair and shoved my face against the wall. "Did I hear you threaten my wife?"

"No."

"So what did I hear?"

"I didn't threaten anyone."

"You think you're special around here?" he shouted. "What makes you think you should be treated any differently than any of the other kids here? Do you think you're better than everyone else?"

"I didn't say that."

"So what are you saying?"

"I just didn't feel like talking to anyone tonight."

"Where were you?"

"I already told you."

"What were you doing in the park?"

"Thinking."

"Thinking about what?"

"My baby," I whispered.

"What were you doing? Were you trying to mess yourself up again? You looking for another unwanted child?"

"I was only sitting on the bench."

"Did you have sex with someone tonight?"

"No."

"Are you sure?"

"I'm sure."

He released me and went over to Nicky. They whispered together for several minutes. Finally, she turned to me and said, "You may go to your room."

I couldn't believe that Leo had used my baby against me. As if I had gone out looking to get pregnant with Christopher! Why was it that every time my baby was mentioned, it always sounded so horrible? I passed my hand along the lower part of my abdomen and felt the scar from the operation.

"Are you all right?" asked Lydia, sitting on my bed.

"I don't know."

"What were they so mad about?"

"I went to the park without permission."

"I'm sorry."

"It's not your fault. The freedom was worth it. I needed to sort out some things in my head. I'd do it again."

"You look awful."

"Thanks, Lydia. That's just what I needed to hear."

I had been tossing and turning for almost an hour, when Nicky quietly came into the room and put something on my dresser. Minutes passed before I felt brave enough to look. There were my diary, purse and cigarettes.

I went to the bathroom and washed my face. My wrist and upper arm were red. I went back to my room and was pulling on my jeans when I heard Lydia say, "What are you doing, Vanessa?"

"I don't know."

"You're going to get in trouble again."

"I know."

"Can I do something?"

"No, Lydia. This is my fight."

"Good luck, Ness."

"I've never once been lucky, Lydia. I doubt if things are going to change now."

"Are you sure that you're all right?"

"Positive." I looked around. "Lydia, when I'm gone, you can help yourself to anything that you want."

She looked at me strangely. I tidied up my dresser, and hung up the stray clothes cluttering my half of the room.

An hour later, at daybreak, I let myself out the back door of the group home for what I hoped would be the last time.

The walk to the lake was cold, and my ears were frozen before I had gone halfway. The bitter wind made my eyes water.

The sky was turning red. I looked at it stretched above the freezing lake. I stood on the shore and willed myself to walk into the water.

I cursed the world and everyone in it. I fell to my knees, plunged my face into the muddy water, beat the ground with my fist until I had blistered my hand.

Why couldn't I just do it?

I had thought about it so many times: coming here, walking out into the lake, and not coming back. Being at peace, away from everyone and everything, free from remembering what had happened, free from wanting my mother's affection. Now I was here, on my knees, dirty lake water mixed with sand covering my face, and I couldn't do it. I couldn't kill myself.

Part II

CHAPTER EIGHTEEN

Walking to the bathroom was a struggle. Every time I moved my legs, I felt like I was being torn apart. The burning feeling worsened as I sat on the toilet. I reached for my compact mirror, and the sight of my reflection confirmed what I was already certain of: I was not being raped again. It was just the dream. The same dream, night after night, month after month, year after year.

It was time I did something about it.

In the morning, I opened the storage closet and got out the box that held the cards and letters I'd received over the years. Without much of a search, I found my old diary.

The dreams had been a lot more explicit and draining since my last visit to my mother's house.

I had been taking a nap in the basement when I felt something between my legs. It was Ralph's hand. I jumped up and looked at him with horror and disgust. "What the hell do you think you're doing?"

He continued to stroke my legs with his fingers. I slapped his hand away and started toward the stairs.

"Relax, Pet."

"Are you fucking crazy?" I screamed.

"No one's home. June's shopping."

"What is that supposed to mean?"

"Come on. Have a drink."

"Ralph, you are the sickest bastard I've ever met."

"You know I love you."

"You love me so much that after all these years you're willing to do this to me again?"

"Pet, you know you want it as much as me."

"What is *wrong* with you?"

"June is so fucking cold. You know I've always loved you. Why did you go and spoil things? You could still be living here, and June wouldn't know a thing. She's so fucking stupid, she believes anything you put in her face."

"How can you talk about her like that?"

"You think I don't know that you and your man were having sex down here last night?"

"That's not true. And even if it was, I've been married since I was sixteen, remember?"

"I could make you feel so good."

"Don't you realize I'm going to tell my mother about this?"

"June will believe anything I tell her. You should know that by now. Anyway, we both know that you didn't come here for no visit. You came because you wanted me to make love to you. You missed me."

"You're so sick, Ralph. Aren't you ever going to change?"

I left my mother's house the next day, without telling her what had happened. I knew that he was right: she would never believe me.

It had taken many years for her and I to start talking to each other again. And we never talked about what had happened to me as a teenager. For me, it was worth it to have a mother. We talked on the phone and sometimes even enjoyed our conversations. There *was* a lingering pain. I always felt like we were being fake, and we were. But somehow, having a fake mother was better than having no mother at all.

No one in my family ever mentioned Christopher. I had the feeling that my brothers didn't remember, or they had blocked it out.

Now I couldn't pretend anymore. Even though I lived only thirty minutes away from my mother, I stopped going to see her. Every time I started to dial her number, I put down the phone. I knew if I talked to her again, I was going to tell her what happened with Ralph — not only what happened recently but what happened almost ten years ago. I had the urge to fill her in on what had been happening in my life since that awful day when he first raped me.

The dreams were getting worse. I always woke up wanting to talk to my mother.

I couldn't remember everything clearly. It's amazing how the mind works. All those years I had managed to keep the memories and hurt at bay, while I fulfilled my desire for work and college. Up until I got married and left the Children's Aid Society, the details of my life were little more than a blur. I knew that I'd been very unhappy. I remembered being in the group homes but no details of my everyday life there. I remembered the first rape, and I remembered the hospital. And I always remembered that I'd had a baby by my stepfather. I never stopped secretly wondering how he died and where he was buried. Now, the person responsible had reminded me of it and my mind was bombarding me with questions. That I was now ten years older than when he raped me worked to my advantage; maybe it was better that I had lived for so long with my memories locked away.

Fragments of information, like bits of a puzzle, started coming together. Before, the few memories I'd had made no sense, and I'd figured they were figments of a not-altogether-healthy mind. There were times when I doubted I'd really been raped by my mother's husband, wondered whether maybe I'd created the distance between my mother and me, wondered whether my dreams were memories or were things I invented in my own mind. But now, everything was starting to make sense.

I read for most of the day, and I wrote down the names of all the people mentioned in the journals that I kept during that time in my life. Next to each name I made a note of the person's significance and what each knew of the circumstances that led to my being placed in the custody of the Children's Aid Society. By late afternoon, I had compiled a long list of people. I hoped they would be willing and able to help me put the pieces together. Then I started to search for the names in the phone book. I managed to find three.

Before phoning my old high school to find out what had happened to Mrs. Sheppard since I left, I dialled the Children's Aid Society. Two years before, I had filed a request for information from their files on me, and I'd requested it again a few weeks ago.

"Ms Alleyne," said the secretary, "I understand your desire for the information from your files. However, I must warn you that we receive hundreds of these requests, and at present we have a tremendous backlog. It may be another six months before we're able to comply with your request. You'll just have to be patient."

"Maybe you didn't understand what I said." I bit my tongue in an effort to control my frustration. "I have written to you three times in the past couple of years. This time, I'm afraid that I am not willing or able to wait another six months. I intend to get that information, *soon*, even if I have to come to Toronto and get it myself."

I listened as she promised that she would get her supervisor to call me as soon as possible, then I put the phone down. With only one month left before 1991, I was still hoping for a new lead before the end of 1990. I'd tried to convince myself that it didn't matter if it took a few more years. After all, I had already waited this long. But I knew it did matter.

CHAPTER NINETEEN

My mind felt like a sheet of paper that had been crumpled and then smoothed out again, with some of the words on it smudged and illegible. Small memories emerged every day. The nightmares had become so real that most nights I jumped out of bed and had to force myself back to reality. I thought I could hear myself crying, only it wasn't the 24-year-old me, it was a young girl. Many mornings, I awoke with monstrous headaches. What was scaring me the most was the lost time. I'd get lost in myself, and when I managed to shake things out I would realize that I had actually blacked out. Sometimes I found myself driving to places I hadn't planned on driving to. I'd wind up at a lake somewhere, usually late at night. Sometimes I had to drive around a bit before I was certain of where I was.

The incidents of the past haunted me, awake or asleep.

When I closed my eyes, I'd see my stepfather's face smiling back at me. Sometimes I even thought I could smell his sweat. One night, after reliving the first rape in yet another vivid nightmare, I slept in the living room for the rest of the night. Early the next morning I phoned Trish.

There had been times in the past when I'd thought I was crazy. After all, everyone around me at the time, adults and police included, had doubted me. The only person who had believed me right from the start and had helped me look forward to another day was my friend Trish. We didn't see much of each other anymore, but Trish had been there for me, and time and distance had not diminished our friendship.

Although Trish had not been able to rescue me from my mother and stepfather, I always appreciated that she at least had wanted to. I'd spent a lot of time at her house. This continued right up to grade eleven, when I moved into a new group home and was taken out of school. She had a large family with both parents, sisters and brothers and a few animals. It reminded me of my family back in Trinidad. Although Trish's family wasn't perfect, they loved each other, and her parents were warm and kind to me.

Trish was just as committed to schoolwork as I was. We shared most of our classes and often studied together. Trish was my only real competition in our typing classes. Soon after I left school, when I'd just turned sixteen, I got married. Of course, it wouldn't have been a wedding at all if Trish hadn't attended. Days later, when I gave birth to my son Josh, Trish was there.

Shortly after, we began to go our separate ways. We went to different colleges. It had been a long time since I had spoken to her. Years, to be sure.

"Hi Trish," I said, trying to sound cheerful. "It's Vanessa. I just came across your number and thought I'd give you a call."

"I haven't seen you since my wedding shower!" Trish sounded excited. We talked for a while. I found out that Trish was finally pregnant. She had wanted a baby for so long.

"To tell you the truth, I've been pretty busy," I said, after a while. "I'm calling because I think I need your help."

Trish was very helpful. She had clear memories of the day after the first rape.

"That was the day we sat in the park, crying together. You were so afraid to go home. Your mother had beaten you when you tried to tell her what happened, and you didn't want to talk to her again."

She remembered other things too: "You were so scared when you found out that you were really pregnant ... That day when Children's Aid took you from school, they brought me to their office and questioned me."

It felt really good having her around to talk to again. I promised to let her know how things were shaping up.

I started to realize that I wasn't the one who should have been afraid. Ralph should have been ashamed to be around people. He should have been forced to face what he had done. I also realized that those people who had known about the abuse were out of my life now. I had cut off contact with them to make it easier to forget. Now, I had to try and track down as many of them as I could. I would be keeping my parents' secret as long as the people who could expose them weren't around. I decided to tell anyone who would listen. I was going to face my past and not be ashamed.

Christmas 1991 came and went. I was absorbed in finding out everything I had forgotten. I decided it was time to start keeping a diary again, to keep track of what I learned or remembered. I bought myself a leather-bound book, and started to write things down.

On January 8, 1992, I got a call from the Metro Children's Aid Society. "I'm not surprised that you've made this request," said the social worker. "Many women find that as they get older they want to find out about things they can't remember. I'm here on a contract position; I've been hired especially to work on the backlog of requests. I get the impression that you need this information immediately. I've spoken to my supervisor, and I'm going to look into your case as soon as I'm finished the one that I'm working on now."

"I appreciate that."

"Well, I don't want to get your hopes up. It may still take a bit of time, and I'll have to look into what information I'm allowed to give you."

"That's okay. As long as you get to it as soon as you can. If things turn out as I suspect they will, I'm going to attempt to press new charges. I may need the information to prove my case."

"I'll keep you posted."

I phoned the police station in my area and described to an officer the incidents that I did remember. For twenty minutes, he listened patiently.

"Do I have any rights with regards to all that happened back then?" I asked.

"As I understand it, you have a right to press new charges if you wish."

There had been some talk in one of my group homes that my stepfather should have been convicted of child molesting, but as far as I knew, nothing had happened after the initial charges were dropped. The idea of having the right to press new charges against him intrigued me. Maybe that would guarantee that Ralph never did it again. I had learned that I was not the first girl he had sexually abused — there had been other incidents. This led me to believe that my stepfather really was sick and should at least be in some sort of counselling. The scary thing was, I had three nieces, all under six years old, and I doubted that any of them could tell anyone if my stepfather did anything inappropriate to them. My mother had convinced the whole family that I had lied about Ralph, so nobody's guard was up. I decided that it was my duty to do whatever I could to press new charges. I'd also get the chance I'd always wanted: the chance to tell a judge what my stepfather did to me. If I managed to get a guilty plea or verdict, bonus.

I phoned 55 Division and got in touch with Detective Small, the sergeant in charge of criminal investigations. I explained the reason for my call and gave as many details about my case as I could. Detective Small wrote down my stepfather's name, then promised to look into it and get back to me.

CHAPTER TWENTY

A small voice in my head was warning me to leave the past in the past. I wondered if it was the voice of logic. Darn, I thought. Logic never even came into play before. Where was logic when I was a young newcomer to this country, alone and afraid? When I was locked up with strangers, forced to live like a criminal? When I felt compelled to search cemeteries for a baby I wasn't sure I'd had? To hell with logic, I decided. I'd continue to work from feelings.

In my dreams my mother was standing by my stepfather as he was hurting me. Calling her was not a good idea. She'd claim that I was only bringing up the past to make trouble. She'd have everyone believing that I wanted to hurt her. She wouldn't listen to me. She definitely wouldn't tell me where she had buried my baby almost ten years ago. I was going to have to find everything out on my own.

Of all the things I was feeling, the strangest was knowing that someone was trapped inside me. I could hear this frightened little girl, distant and pleading. She just wanted to come out, to be set free, to rest, but she was afraid that no one would believe her, and so she was hiding. I wanted to comfort her. I'd give her a chance to speak, and then she'd see that things were going to get better.

The idea of just packing up and leaving Canada occurred to me more than once. I had no good memories of Canada, and I figured this proved that this country could never really be my home. I was a citizen, but I felt like an intruder. Making a life for myself in Trinidad couldn't be as difficult as trying to stabilize my life here. I realized that race really wasn't supposed to matter here, but I wondered whether things would be better, or at least easier, if I was White.

Waiting for the call from Detective Small the next morning was one of the hardest things I'd done in a very long time. I picked up the phone a few times and had to force myself to put it down. Wait, wait, wait. I busied myself making coffee, cleaning up the house, browsing through my diary and looking at pictures. I wanted so much to do this right. I didn't want to make any mistakes. I wondered whether I would be in a better position now if I had taken the time to find out all the details about the case ten years ago.

Flipping through an old photo album, I came across a picture of my grandmother, sitting in front of her house, the house I grew up in. I missed her. She had such a beautiful smile, it made the rest of her light up. On her head she wore the customary headtie, knotted on top in one of the African-Caribbean styles she wore so well. I can hardly remember a day in my short life with her that her head was not covered. I have come to believe that this was mostly out of religious conviction. In this picture my grandmother had on a long floral dress that reached to her ankles. That was another custom of hers. I can't remember ever seeing her wear anything that was cut much higher than her ankles.

This was the woman who had taught me to be me, the Grams who listened to me talk about anything and everything. When everyone told me to shut up, she made time to listen. God, to be in the arms of my grandmother at this very moment!

But even my grandmother didn't think that I should take this any further. I'd had a very disturbing phone conversation with her a few years earlier, not long after my visit to Trinidad. I'd found out that my mother had told my child care worker that my grandmother had said I was a troubled child who had caused a lot of problems for her in Trinidad. I was hurt and angry at my grandmother. With all she knew, why was she taking my mother's side? As I'd dialled Grams's number in Trinidad, I felt an ache in my chest that I had only felt one other time — on the day when I tried to tell my mother I'd been raped, and she gave me the beating of my life.

"How yuh could do that to me?" I'd demanded, as soon as my grandmother answered the phone. "I use to trust you more than anybody else in mih whole life. Yuh jes like mih mother. You doh really love me!"

I'd listened to her soft breathing on the other end of the line. A part of me had wanted to reach out to her and tell her I didn't believe anything I'd heard. Another part of me was too hurt to stop. "You lie! You take she side although yuh know ah was telling de truth."

She had listened to me without interrupting. I was beginning to think she wasn't going to respond, when finally she answered. "Pet," she'd said, lingering on the name she herself had given me. "I don't know what yuh talkin' about. What I say to hurt yuh so much that yuh talkin' to mih like dis?"

"You cyah even tell de truth. You jes like all the rest. You is a liar and I hate you. I doh ever want to talk to yuh again!" Without giving her a chance to reply, I slammed down the phone.

Now, looking at her picture in my photo album, I thought about how I'd stopped writing to her, and how the little money I'd been sending her from time to time had also stopped. I had made a few trips to Trinidad since, but although neither of us ever mentioned that conversation, it was never forgotten. I was always careful what I said to her on the phone.

I couldn't remember why I had been so angry at her. She had sided with her own daughter — wasn't that what I wanted my own mother to do? God, how complicated life got.

I closed my eyes and tried to remember the good times with my grandmother. I smiled as I recalled our days in her little garden, picking flowers for the altar in our small church. I remembered the congregation gathering every Sunday. I'd loved the way the older Black folks sounded when they sang. The men's voices were calm and deep, while the women brought out powerful tones from deep within themselves. I remembered each face clearly. The glorious melodies of the old spirituals would rise slowly, filling the church, lingering in the air. My grandmother would be sitting in her special seat at the left-hand side, near the front. Everyone else would be standing, except for a few toddlers squatting on the benches that lined the aisle. I was back in Trinidad, with my aunts and cousins. It was Sunday again. Everything was back to normal.

My grandmother's distinctive voice filled the church. I looked up at her face and tried to make my own squeaky voice match hers. Everyone was clapping and beating tambourines in a rhythm that forced your feet to move. The two small drums created a feeling of ritual and calm. Then the chorus began. All of us children waited patiently for the chorus, sometimes the only part of the song we could remember. Now the whole congregation would be singing, 'I'll fly away...' The flowers my grandmother and I had picked earlier that day added a beauty to the church, and the candles made patterns on the wall, the patterns sometimes moving as if they were dancing in time with the music.

Sometimes, when I did a really good job of polishing the benches in the church or shining the brass, my grandmother would let me read a few verses from the Bible. I felt so special, standing in front of grown-ups and reading, that I daydreamed about maybe becoming a preacher or a nun when I grew up. Maybe I could even be a missionary. One time in particular I remember sharing my dreams for the future with my grandmother.

"When ah get big and rich ah going to build a big house with a special section for you, Grams."

"Yuh saying dat now, but when yuh get big yuh going to forget all bout me," she answered playfully.

"Ah mean it. You is de best grandmother in de whole world. Ah going to take care of you forever," I insisted.

"I know yuh will, Pet."

I sat with Grams, talking and brushing her hair.

Pulling myself back to reality, I found that I had wasted the whole morning daydreaming. I checked my answering machine to make sure that I hadn't missed the phone call from Detective Small, then I made myself a cup of coffee and sat down near the phone, a cigarette in my mouth waiting to be lighted. I called the detective myself.

"I'm a bit anxious for the information I requested from you," I explained.

Before I got any further, he told me, "Ms. Alleyne, I have the information in front of me. The case was originally investigated by this department. Correct me if I'm wrong. I'm just going to read you the notes I have here."

I heard him flipping through some paper, and I took out my new black leather journal. I opened it to a fresh page and sat alert, pen in one hand and cigarette in the other. He began to read. "On May 19, 1983, one Ralph Godfrey was arrested and brought to the station, where charges were filed against him. This was due to a complaint received from the Children's Aid Society regarding an alleged assault on a fourteen-year-old, identified as his stepdaughter, one Vanessa Alleyne. He appeared in court on June 7, 1983. On September 6, 1983, the charges were withdrawn by the Crown."

"Why were the charges withdrawn?"

"I don't have that information here. The person who did the original investigation was Sergeant Wood. He's now the Sergeant in charge of training at 14 Division. If you want to know anything else, I recommend that you contact him, since he's the one who was actually there."

"Do you know who the Crown Attorney was?"

"No, ma'am. I'm afraid you'll have to contact Sergeant Wood to find that out."

Why would the Crown Attorney have withdrawn charges? It didn't make any sense to me. I decided to contact this Sergeant Wood immediately.

"I'm sorry that I'm not able to help you much," he told me when I reached him on the phone. "Nineteen eighty-three was a long time ago, and I've investigated so many similar cases, it's really hard to remember one in particular."

Trying not to sound desperate, I asked, "Don't you take notes on cases that you're in charge of investigating?"

"I'll check my old notes. I can't promise you that I still have them, but I'll see what I can come up with."

"When can I expect to hear from you?"

"Give me your number, and I'll get in touch with you as soon as possible."

CHAPTER TWENTY-ONE

A round the same time, I learned something that might allow me to solve another mystery in my life. I was talking to a relative I'd kept in touch with. He asked me, "Would it make a difference in your life if you'd known your real father , Pet?"

"I don't know," I said thoughtfully. "I used to think it would. But the closest thing to a father I ever had was my stepfather, and that didn't turn out so great."

"Would you like to know who your father is?"

The excitement I felt when he said this took me by surprise.

"Why? Do you know who he is?"

"Has your mother ever said anything to you about someone named Paul Turnbull?"

"No, who's Paul Turnbull?"

"He was your mother's first boyfriend. He has a twin brother by the name of Peter who went out with your Aunt Daisy."

"Does he live in Trinidad?"

"Last I heard, he'd moved to New York. But that was over twenty years ago."

Filled with curiosity, I decided to call Ted, a friend of mine who did some detective work part-time. Ted was very special to me. We'd met in his taxi, on the night I left my husband.

When I was sixteen, all that mattered to me was getting out of the clutches of the Children's Aid Society. Getting married seemed like an easy escape. The fact that my husband-to-be was in love with me made the choice easier. So did the fact that the church we both belonged to made it hard just to date and get to know each other. When I found out that I was pregnant with Josh, I was stunned. I'd never dreamed that I'd be able to have kids after that awful operation. While in group homes, I'd learned that the only ways to break a Crown wardship were to have a baby or get married. I was only too happy that both were happening at once.

My husband seemed vulnerable and needy. I felt that by being there for him, I was rescuing him. Of course, I also hoped he'd be there for me, too. But I learned early on that when I'd married him, I'd also married all his problems, and his whole family's problems as well.

One day, when we'd been married for two years, things came to a head. During the afternoon, while I was at work, my husband beat little Josh for leaving his toys on the bedroom floor. When I got home, Josh was so hurt and scared that he could barely tell me what had happened. I confronted my husband. He was so offended that I would question his judgement that he beat me too. He must have knocked me unconscious because when I came to my senses, Josh was crying and yelling at his father to leave his mommy alone.

I crawled to the phone and called the police. I whispered into the mouthpiece that my husband was hurting my son. Then I pulled myself up off the floor and went over to Josh. I pulled him away from his father, hating that man more than I remembered hating anyone but my stepfather. I took my son to his room, and locked us both in. Sitting on the bottom bunk, I cradled him and kissed away his tears. "Don't cry, baby. Mommy's all right ... Mommy's not going to let anyone hurt you ever again ... Don't cry, Joshie ... Mommy's here ... "

I knew what I had to do. I couldn't wait for this to happen again. One of the first things I had learned in my college psychology class was that a man who hits you once will most likely hit you again.

There was a knocking on the bedroom door. I didn't answer it at first — I waited until I was sure it was the police.

Putting Josh down on the bed, I got up and opened the door. Standing in front of me were two police officers.

"You called?" the taller of the two asked, chewing gum and blowing small bubbles.

"Yes I did. My husband assaulted both my son and me. He knocked me out for a few seconds. I want you to press charges."

The tall officer turned and called my husband over.

"Did you hit your wife and your son?"

My husband nodded. "I'm sorry," he said quietly.

"Look, he said he was sorry," said the tall officer. "Why don't you guys try to work things out? If he hits you again, call us." He turned to go.

"I just told you that he assaulted my son and me! Look at my face and my arms!" I showed them my bruises and scratches.

"Why don't we take him away from here, and maybe when you both cool off tomorrow you can talk things out?"

"I don't want to talk things out," I shouted, "I want him arrested!"

Five minutes later, my husband left with the two police officers. They took him outside, and told him not to come within a hundred feet of the apartment for the night.

Thirty minutes later, I had a suitcase filled with the baby's clothes, a few things of my own, and all our important papers. My passport and our birth certificates I put in my purse. I packed my son's bottles and diaper and some snacks. Before long, Josh and I were sitting in a taxi. Where we were going, I had no idea. All I knew was that we were not coming back.

I asked the driver to head for downtown Toronto. Through the taxi window, I scanned the area for my husband. Having reassured myself that he wasn't around and hadn't seen us leave, I began some mental calculations. With the pay check I would receive the next day and the money I had in the bank, I should be all right for a while. Thank God for my grandmother's advice. I had my own bank account, my private money for emergencies. After all, your husband doesn't need to know everything about you.

"So where are we going?" asked the driver.

"I'm not sure." I thought for a minute. "Do you think you can find me a motel or something downtown?"

"Why would you want to go to a motel with your little baby?"

"I'm leaving my husband and I have no place else to go."

"What about your family? You must be able to go to your family's house."

"I don't get along much better with my family than I do with my husband, I'm afraid."

"Would you like a drink or something?"

"No thank you."

"How about a cup of coffee?"

"Thanks, that would be nice."

He pulled up to the drive-through window of a McDonalds and ordered two coffees and, for Josh, a small order of fries.

"My name is Ted," he told me, pulling into a parking spot at a nearby park. "What's yours?"

"Vanessa."

"Let's sit on the bench for awhile," Ted suggested, opening the door on Josh's side of the car. "It's not so dark, and you two look like you need some fresh air."

I realized for the first time that night just how big a man he really was. When he sat at the wheel of his taxi, his head almost touched the roof. He was a good-looking Black man, perhaps in his early forties. His voice was deep and comforting, and his eyes were almost black. He was a shade darker than me and spoke with an accent that sounded kind of English, with a West Indian flavour.

I got out of the car slowly, watching this stranger holding my son as if they were friends. He placed Josh's blanket on the grass and put the fries on it. Without making a sound, Josh sat down and started eating the fries.

We sat on a bench, and Ted took out a pack of cigarettes from his pocket and offered me one. I hadn't had a smoke since I found out I was pregnant. Now, I took the cigarette with gratitude and closed my eyes with the first drag. It was a bit uncomfortable at first, but with each drag it got easier. I felt a lot more at ease than I had when I got into the taxi.

Three hours later, I had agreed to stay at Ted's place for the night while he finished his shift. The next day he helped me find an apartment.

Now, armed with information I thought might lead me to my real father, I called Ted.

"Well, look who the storm blew in," said Ted.

"Sorry I haven't been in touch." Briefly, I attempted to explain my four-year absence.

"How are my kids?"

"Don't you just wish!"

We joked around for a while, then I said, "I want your help finding some information about a person living in New York. He might know who my father is."

"So you won't let me close to my kids, but you want me to help you find your father?"

"Why don't you try making some kids of your own, if you love mine so much?"

"Well, I have a little boy. He's almost three."

"So now that you have your own, are you ready to leave mine alone?"

"We'll see. Now, how about giving me the person's name? I'll see what I can do."

CHAPTER TWENTY-TWO

Coming up with a case against my stepfather was not going to be as difficult as I'd once thought. Even if the statute of limitation had changed for sexual abuse, it probably wouldn't affect me. I was almost certain that I could at least get a justice of the peace to hear me out.

I was writing up some notes in my journal when the phone rang. It was the social worker from the Children's Aid Society. "You sound a bit calmer today," she said. "I hope the information I have here is helpful."

She had my attention. "It's something that will at least make sense to me, I hope," I said.

"Well, Vanessa, according to your files here, the case was actually withdrawn from court due to — and I quote — 'your emotional state and vulnerability at the time of the case, the fact that the allegations were filed too late, and lastly, the fact that your mother had made it clear that she was in full support of your stepfather' — that apparently made it too difficult to try." I waited for her to continue, my hand busily writing down as much of the conversation as I could.

"It says here that you and a representative from the Children's Aid Society met with the Crown attorney and decided it would be in your best interest to withdraw the case."

"I can't remember agreeing to that."

"Judging from the state you seem to have been in back then, I'm surprised you remember anything at all."

"Wasn't it the Children's Aid Society's job to make sure that those things were explained to me, so that I at least understood what was going on?"

"I really don't know."

"Do you know who the crown attorney was?"

"I don't see it here. I could look it up."

"I would really appreciate it. I don't think that I have a choice but to press new charges."

As I put the phone down, I muttered to myself, "Someone had better have some answers."

I waited around that day and the next for a call from Sergeant Wood, then decided to call him myself.

"I have the notes here," he said, as soon as he heard my voice. "I remember the case now. Your mother said that you were very active sexually, and there was something about an abortion."

"I don't know anything about an abortion or about me being sexually active. I was fourteen years old, for Christ's sake!"

"My guess is that the case was probably withdrawn due to lack of evidence. I don't have a follow-up."

"Could you back up for a minute?" I was not quite sure what I was being told. "I had a child for my stepfather just a little over four months before you started your investigation. What more evidence did the police need?"

"I don't have anything here stating that you had a child by the accused."

"But wasn't the baby the reason that I was taken into the care of the Children's Aid Society and for the charges against my stepfather?"

"As far as I can see, we received a report from someone at the Children's Aid Society. We followed up on it, and as a result your stepfather, Ralph Godfrey, was arrested. I don't have any other information."

"Under the circumstances, I would like to press new charges. As a matter of fact, I would like to know exactly why nothing else was done about this. I'm going to look into what should have happened and what actually happened. I'll be in touch with you, Sergeant Wood."

I hung up and lit another cigarette. God, how screwed up the whole darn Canadian justice system was! Why the hell did the police even bother to lay charges against Ralph if they didn't intend to follow through with a proper investigation? Just like the Children's Aid Society, the police department jumped in and changed my whole life, then backed off and left me holding the pieces. And my own mother. How could she tell the police that I was a slut? Shit, I'd never even fully kissed a boy at that age!

Later, as I was preparing for bed, I decided that though I couldn't force my mother to love me, I could force her to recognize how her actions had affected me. If I did get the case to court, she would undoubtedly support my stepfather again. But this time I'd be strong enough to handle her decision. If things worked out the way I hoped, my mother would have to testify, if not in support of her husband, then at least as a hostile witness. And it would be worth going to court, worth being questioned and cross-examined if my mother would finally listen to me. My only fear was that the justice system might let me down again. Would the job be done this time? Would justice finally be served?

If I succeeded, I'd send the message that those of us who have been sexually abused are not going to remain silent forever. I wanted to let Canada know that being sexually abused is not like getting the flu: We can't take some medicine, put on a few Band-Aids and go on with our lives. We need more than a few sessions of counselling. We need to be listened to and heard throughout the many difficult phases of our healing.

The next day I contacted the Victim/Witness Coordinator at the Crown's office.

"I want something done right away. I have this awful feeling that if I don't get on this right away, I'll be lost in the system like before," I explained. "I can't let that happen again."

"From what you've said, you've actually done an excellent job so far."

"What else can I do?"

"The next thing that you should do is to let the Detective in charge set up a date for you to go down to the station and make your statement. Are you ready for that?"

"Yes, I think I am."

"After you've made your statement, it'll probably take a little while before the police lay the new charges. Once they lay the charges, your stepfather will be arrested. Judging from the fact that your mother has always supported him fully, I would think that as soon as his bail is set, she'll post it for him."

"Where am I while this is all taking place?"

"You won't be involved at this point," the coordinator explained. "Your stepfather will have to appear in court to set a date for the trial. The trial will take place at Old City Hall or College Park Court. The system is so backed up that his first court appearance probably won't happen until August or even a bit later."

"Should I contact a lawyer?"

"The Crown will represent you. You'll get a summons when all the paperwork has been taken care of. I'd say the actual trial will probably happen sometime next year."

"What are my chances of actually getting this case heard?"

"Very good. I've seen women take their abusers to court after more than twenty-five years and win. Nine years isn't really as long as it sounds when you consider that many victims can't talk about the abuse even a lifetime after it happened. You're very strong to be taking such a stand."

"I'm afraid that while I feel a lot of things, somehow, strong isn't one of them."

"As long as you're aware that the road you're about to travel isn't an easy one, you'll be just fine."

"I'm just hoping that I'm not opening a door that should really remain shut. But I need to find some peace of mind, and I won't be able to until I am absolutely sure that my stepfather will never do it again. I want him to take responsibility for what he did to me."

"I understand. If you keep me up to date on what's happening, I'll be able to help you prepare for court. Remember that the small steps, like the one you're taking, are what will eventually allow sexual abuse to be brought out into the open. Good luck with everything."

"I hope that I'm not going to be needing luck. I'm hoping the justice system will work this time."

CHAPTER TWENTY-THREE

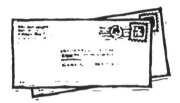

I wanted to have all the information I needed in front of me before I took my case any further. Over the next few weeks, I got in touch with my old group homes, my old case workers at the Children's Aid Society, the social worker who had reported my case to the police, and anyone else I could track down.

I was in the middle of one of those phone calls when a package from the Children's Aid Society arrived for me. As I held it in my hands, I saw it was marked personal and confidential, and I started to shake with excitement. It took all my concentration to walk back over to the sofa and sit down. I lit a cigarette, opened the envelope, and began to read.

Dear Vanessa

I am writing in response to your request for a complete history of yourself while in our care ... I hope this letter is able to provide you with the details that you need in order to help you in your process of healing ... Our agency first had contact with your family in May 1983 after receiving information that you had made sexual abuse allegations against your stepfather ... You, your mother, social worker, and teacher were interviewed by the police ... Your stepfather was later seen at home by police and taken to the station where he was formally charged with sexual assault ... Your mother and stepfather continued to deny allegations of abuse ...

Our decision to place you in care was based on our determination that you were in need of protection ... you were apprehended by our society and placed in an emergency foster home ... Crown Wardship was obtained in September, 1983 ... we were your legal guardians and therefore responsible for your well-being until you reached the age of majority ... Our records indicate that on September 6, 1983, you had a meeting with the Crown attorney in Criminal Court ... the Crown decided not to proceed with the charges against your stepfather because: 1) they felt that you were too emotionally fragile to withstand court proceedings. 2) they had little evidence, and 3) the allegations were filed too late ...

While at the foster home it became apparent that you were emotionally distraught ... you needed to be in a more structured environment to help you work out your feelings about the sexual abuse allegations, the loss of your baby, as well as your feelings associated with your mother and stepfather's denial of the abuse ... You were in a great deal of distress, and there were concerns about your suicidal ideation ... Initially, you were assessed by a consultant psychiatrist and found to be depressed and preoccupied with suicide ... you were seen by the Clarke Institute of Psychiatry ... You completed the "Sexual Abuse meetings" ... were referred to two incest survival therapists to help deal with the aftermath of sexual abuse ...

I read the letter over three times before moving on to the report from the Hospital for Sick Children. It contained a detailed explanation of why my baby died.

Premature lungs and water in his abdomen were listed as the main factors. He also had cysts on his right kidney, attributed to an abnormal gene passed on to him by both me and my stepfather. Apparently that was minor and could have been corrected with surgery, but the hospital where he was born hadn't been equipped to deal with it, or with his prematurity. He had been delivered by Caesarian section because he was a breach birth and because he was already in distress when my mother took me to the hospital. The report seemed to suggest that he might have lived if I had gotten proper medical care during my pregnancy. Had my mother denied me that care in the hopes that the baby would die, leaving no proof of what her husband had done to me?

In tears, I slipped off the sofa and onto the floor. My body curled into a ball and I began the rocking that usually accompanied my crying sessions. Sometimes I'd finish crying and be unable to recall why I'd started in the first place. Often, I was left with a heavy feeling in my chest, as if the pain was stuck there and refused to come out.

Today, the pressure in my chest left me short of breath. The strength I had felt only hours before was gone, and I felt like a lonely and desperate child. I wanted to run and hide. I always felt like that just before I blacked out. It had happened five times, and each time, I had been thinking about my past just before it happened. I managed to pull myself up and talk myself over to the phone.

"You're fine ... Nothing bad is happening to you ... You're at home in the living room and you're not hurt ... Nobody can hurt you here ... Call someone... Just pick up the phone and call for help ... You're all right ... Call the Rape Crisis Centre ... You can do it ... "

"I need to speak to someone right away," I heard myself say.

"I can have someone call you right back. I just need your name and number."

"When will I hear from you?"

"In a few minutes."

I gave my name and number and curled up in the corner near the phone. A few minutes later, it rang.

"This is Bev calling from the Rape Crisis Centre. Is this Vanessa?"

"Yes."

"You wanted a number for an incest survivors' group. I could put your name on the list, but there's a very long waiting period."

"I'm going crazy right now," I cried. "If I wait any longer I won't need a group, I'll need a mental hospital."

"Why don't you tell me what's bothering you? Maybe I can help with some of it."

"I don't know what's wrong with me. I'm feeling very anxious and unsure."

"Have you been raped or assaulted?"

"Nine years ago," I said. "That's why I don't understand what's going on."

"That's not strange at all, Vanessa. A lot of survivors find it hard to live with those terrible memories."

"Why don't you tell me how many people you know of who get up at night feeling like they're being raped? Who get up swearing that they're bleeding or bruised? I feel these things. I think I'm losing it."

"There are a lot of us out there. These things happen every day. You'd be surprised how many women are going through exactly what you're experiencing. It takes time to deal with all that's happened to you. Remember that rape is a very traumatic event. No matter how old or young you are when it happens, you normally end up feeling the same way. You just have to learn how to use those experiences to make you a stronger and happier person. Things get better. You've started to go through the healing process. It's hard, but in the long run you'll see that it's actually good for you."

"I don't see how feeling the way I do is suppose to be good for me."

"Look at it this way. If your mind didn't think that you were finally ready to deal with these experiences, it would probably keep the memories hidden. By allowing you to face the memories, your mind is actually telling you that it's time you took care of yourself and dealt with your past."

"When am I going to be able to deal with these strange emotions? They just seem to come and go without any control."

"I don't think they ever really go away. We just have to learn new ways of dealing with them."

"The thing I'd most like to get under control are these crying spells."

"What part of your experiences is bothering you the most?"

"The baby." I felt a bit foolish that I was still bothered by it. "I still don't know where they buried my baby. I can't stop wondering where he is or who was there when he died. I don't even know whether he died alone." I paused to blow my nose and wipe away my tears. "He died while I was asleep in the hospital. My mother took care of all the arrangements and never told me anything about it. I couldn't bring myself to ask her. She refused to admit that the baby was for my stepfather."

"Why not ask her now? You have a right to know where your child is buried."

"I haven't spoken to her for over a year. Last time I visited her, my stepfather made sexual advances towards me again. After I left her house, my nightmares started to get more frequent and more vivid. That's one of the main reasons I decided to file charges. I knew that if I told her, she would automatically take his side, so I decided to deal with him myself."

"How do you feel about your mother now?"

"Over the years, I've maintained contact with her. I just pretended that she did love me and that the things my stepfather did weren't really that important. Now, I'm finally facing the fact that she was partly to blame for my abuse, at least for the fact that it went on for as long as it did. I guess I'm really disappointed and angry at her. It's almost like she expects me to forget I had the baby. Maybe she thinks that if I don't know where he's buried, it's easier for me to forget."

"You have a right to feel the way you do. You have to stop protecting her. She should have been there for you when you were being raped by her husband."

"She doesn't see things that way. Every time I try to bring it up, she says I'm just hell-bent on making trouble for her. You know, this is the first time that I feel like I really don't care whether she approves of me or not. I feel like I must do something."

"What do you think will happen if you succeed in filing charges against your stepfather?"

"The way I see it, either she'll try to make up for everything, or she'll finally disown me once and for all. I could live with either outcome. What I can't live with is being in the middle. And I'd really like to know what was going on in her mind, how she managed to live with my stepfather and continue sleeping with him for all these years."

"She probably blocked out everything the same way you did. She may even be thinking about it as much as you do. You just never know what's on her mind. You have to keep hoping that one day she'll face the truth. What's important now is that you get help for yourself. You have to make yourself well before you start trying to deal with your mother's problems. Maybe one day you'll be able to talk to each other about what happened."

Another five minutes and I was off the phone, feeling a lot better. Having someone on my side made me feel strong enough to pick up where I left off.

CHAPTER
TWENTY-FOUR

Early in January 1992, I came up against another obstacle in my search to find out where my baby was buried. The hospital where I had given birth sent me to its medical records department, but the woman in charge there refused to help me.

"You do realize that I'm now an adult and entitled to whatever records you have concerning myself?" I said, frustrated. "I was told that I'd be able to get the information if I came down here myself."

"I'm sorry, but we are not covered under the new Freedom of Information Act. You'll have to go through your family doctor to get access to the records."

The drive from Toronto to Whitby usually took forty minutes, but it seemed to take hours today. Back in my apartment at last, I decided to call Bev at the Rape Crisis Centre. Maybe I'd get a few ideas from her. Since our first conversation, I had come to rely on the kind and understanding words of Bev. We had never met, but I felt I could trust her. It was nice having someone to discuss my journey with. It was a lot harder trying to hold things together when I had no one to confide in. I had a few close friends, but there were plenty of problems with confiding in them. They had their own problems, which they couldn't help but share with me, and I doubted that they'd know what to say, or how to act, if they ever found out about my past. Having someone who knew how to help was good.

Bev was surprised to hear what had happened. "What do you mean, you have to get your doctor to request the information?"

"I was hoping *you'd* know. It's really frustrating. I'm being shut out again. When I was fourteen, they said I was too young. Now I'm almost twenty-four, and I still have no rights."

"Have you tried going down to McDonald Block on Bay Street?"

"No … What can they do?"

"They have documents on file for every birth that's registered. Your mother would have needed to get a burial certificate in order to bury your baby. If they received a burial certificate, then they must have had to register him. In most cases the name of the cemetery and funeral home would be listed on the burial certificate. You never know."

"I'll be in Toronto again next week. I could try that, and see if it works out … There's something else I've been thinking about trying. It's a long shot, but so is everything so far. I'll let you know what I come up with."

I said goodbye to her, then reached for the grey plastic bag with the two phone books I had picked up during my trip to Toronto. I took out the Yellow Pages and found the list of funeral homes in the Greater Toronto Area.

Sergeant Wood had no record of the baby, so if I took the case to the detective in charge now, there would be no record that I'd had a child for my stepfather. I figured that if I found the child, it would be much easier for me to prove that I had been sexually abused. This time, I wanted my stepfather to have to face the pressure of proving that the child I had was not his. If I could prove that the baby *was* his, that in itself would prove that he'd had sexual intercourse with me. If I found the baby, then with DNA testing I was positive I could at least prove that.

The idea of calling the funeral homes had come to me on my way to the hospital. If the hospital hadn't prepared the baby for burial, then it must have been done by a funeral home. It would have been a funeral home close to the hospital, since it wouldn't have made a lot of sense to go to one that was far away. The hospital knew nothing about the baby after its death and autopsy, but I figured the funeral home would.

The calls quickly became routine. I would begin by saying that I had been very sick at the time of the death and had not been involved in the burial. I explained that I wanted to pay my respects and was trying to find out where my child was buried. I gave the particulars: a baby boy, a few hours old, my maiden name was Alleyne, my mother's name was Godfrey. Yes, she made the arrangements. Yes, she would have signed the burial certificate. Yes, that was January 23, 1983.

Time after time they checked their records. Time after time they had buried no baby boy on or around that date.

Finally, almost two hours later, I was down to the last two funeral homes that could have prepared Christopher for burial. The secretary at one promised to look up the information and call back with the results. At the other, a woman had to find out if she was allowed to give out such information.

I had done all I could for the time being. I would try Bev's idea next and see if it got me anywhere.

CHAPTER TWENTY-FIVE

Getting ready for a trip to Toronto had also become routine. I'd make sure that I had enough extra cash in my purse, just in case. I'd also throw in my map and two dollars in quarters for the phone calls I was sure to be making. I had an extra cushion which I usually put behind my neck when it got stiff when I was driving; I'd put it on the sofa so I wouldn't forget to take it. Also important was my black book, with the phone numbers and addresses of my friends who lived in Toronto. I tried to make a habit of looking up my friends when I was in the area.

The trip I was preparing for on January 20, 1992, was very important to me. I was going to find out if I could get a death certificate from the Office of the Registrar General. When Bev had first suggested this to me the week before, I wasn't sure if it was worth trying. But a few days ago she'd told me that the reason I was finding it so difficult to get my baby's death off my mind was that it wasn't really final for me. Not getting a chance to see the baby after his death had cheated me of my grief, trapped me in the past. Getting the legal documents relating to the child, maybe even finding out where he was buried, would let me close that chapter. Gaining control over my emotions was enough of a prize to make me want to try.

I hurried around the apartment, making sure I hadn't forgotten anything. I made sure I had written down the name of the doctor who'd delivered the baby, the date and time of the birth, the approximate time of the baby's death, and the name I told my mother I wanted to give him.

Just as I was about to shut the door, the telephone began to ring. I let it ring a few times as I tried to decide whether to put down all the stuff I was carrying and answer it. Finally, I did. By doing so, I made that day one of the most memorable of my life.

"Yes?" I said into the receiver, trying to hold on to the things in my arms.

A man's voice said, "May I speak to Ms Alleyne please."

"You are speaking to her," I put down my purse and the extra cushion.

"I'm calling from Glover Funeral Home. I have some information you requested a little while ago."

"Please hold on." Dropping the rest of what I was holding, I grabbed my purse and got out my cigarettes. I picked up the black notebook with all the information I had gathered over the past months, opened it to the page where I'd written down everything I'd learned so far about the baby and prepared to take notes.

"Thank you for waiting. Please tell me what you've found."

"We did look after an infant for burial on January 26, 1983. Toronto East Hospital was the hospital of birth."

I felt my knees go weak. "Do you think that it was my son? I mean, is my name there?"

"I don't know, but I can tell you that the infant was buried at Pine Hills Cemetery in Scarborough."

Sitting on the floor, I wrote this down. "Thank you," I told him.

There was a possibility that it wasn't my child, but this was the closest I'd come to finding the cemetery. I sat motionless for a few minutes, looking at what I'd written. Had I finally found him? Was this my baby?

I hesitated before phoning the cemetery, but finally my need to confirm my findings overrode my fear of disappointment. I pulled the Toronto phone directory from under the coffee table. Finding the phone number wasn't hard. I wrote it in my black book, lit another cigarette and dialled.

"Pine Hills Cemetery, may I help you?"

"I'd like some information on a baby buried at your cemetery. I believe it's my son, and I'm hoping that you'll be able to confirm it from your files."

"Your son?" the man asked, sounding a bit confused.

"Yes. It's a long story, but if you can look up the name, it would be really helpful."

"What's the last name and date of burial?"

"My last name is Alleyne." I spelled it for him. "But would you also check under Godfrey? He was born on January 23, 1983. I believe the funeral would have been on or about January 26, 1983."

"Just a moment." He put me on hold.

Christ … After all these years I might finally get some solid proof that I was not a nutcase.

A few minutes later, a woman picked up the phone.

"You wanted information on a burial?"

"Yes."

"Was that January 26, 1983?"

"Yes."

"We did have a common burial for an infant boy, Baby Alleyne, Christopher, on January 26, 1983. The grave is in section 11, lot number 2424."

Hearing someone else say "Christopher Alleyne" out loud gave me goosebumps. Until now, I had been the only one to say it. He was *real.* I *did* have a baby. It *wasn't* a dream. My mother did give him the name I asked her to give him. She had actually done something I'd asked for. For so many years I'd searched for him. Now I'd found him simply by phoning funeral homes and asking a few questions. My child's grave was less than an hour away from where I lived.

"Are you there?" asked the woman.

"Yes. I was just writing that down. How can I find the grave?"

"When you get here, just look for numbers marking the different sections. Section 11 is right at the front of the cemetery. There's no marker on the grave. Look on the ground for metal plates with numbers on them. This section is mostly infants, and the graves make a circle. Follow the markers until you find the number 2424, and that's it."

"The name isn't on there?"

"No. Like I said, the grave belongs to Social Services. You're welcome to come into the office and get any other information you need. I hope I was of some help."

"Thank you." I put the phone down gently.

Nine years after losing a child I never thought I could love, I was going to keep my promise.

I remembered seeing him lying there with wires and tubes all over his tiny body. The strange swelling of his stomach was clear in my memory. Yet, although I could recall each of his features, I had somehow lost the image of his whole face. I couldn't remember when it had slipped away, but it was gone. I had often wished that someone had taken a picture of him for me. Even if I hadn't been allowed to see it right away, it would have made my life a lot simpler, soothing my mind during the times I doubted the birth.

CHAPTER TWENTY-SIX

Three hours later, I was standing in the office of Pine Hills Cemetery. Lo and behold: the cemetery was about ten minutes away from my old apartment. Only minutes away, and I'd had no idea.

January 20, 1992, three days short of the ninth anniversary of the birth, I got out of the grey Oldsmobile I had been driving for the past few years and stood leaning against it. The winter wind froze my ears immediately, and my fingers and the rest of my face followed shortly afterwards. I looked up at the sky and thanked God for leading me there. Rain was falling again turning the snow into icy slush.

I looked at the rows of headstones that went on and on. The snow was quite high and I realized that finding a small number on the ground would be impossible today. Instead of being disappointed, I found that a sense of relief came over me. I didn't think that I was ready to stand near the grave. I just wanted to make sure that there was no mistake, that I could stop looking.

Being careful not to slip, I made my way to the office and introduced myself to the manager.

"At present it's still possible to purchase the grave," he told me, "but if another grave is put on top, which usually happens after a number of years, you won't be able to buy it."

"Why would you put another grave on top?"

"After a while we run out of room, and we have no choice. The

next of kin are given ample time to decide whether they wish to purchase the plot or leave it in Social Services' possession. In your case,
there may be some complications. You see, your mother is down as
the infant's next of kin, and I'm afraid you cannot purchase the plot
without her written consent."

"Look," I said. "I had this child when I was fourteen years old, and
at that time I was too young to decide anything for myself. I was raped
and had no choice. When the baby died, I was healing from the operation that brought him into the world, and couldn't attend his funeral. For years, I wondered where he was buried and cried because I
didn't know.

"Now I'm here, and I'm a lot stronger. I am going to be the owner
of my child's grave. I'm not able to get permission from my mother,
and I don't want her to know that I am making these arrangements.
It's my right as the baby's mother." I took a deep breath. "Please contact someone in authority and see what arrangements can be made. I
have all day if it's necessary."

The manager sat on a chair facing me. He looked interested
in what I was saying.

"I'll make a few calls and let you know if there is anything that we
can do." He got up from his chair and went out of the office.

Alone in the office, I allowed myself to shed the tears I didn't
dare let a stranger see. I walked over to the window and looked out at
the front gates of the cemetery. For a long time now I'd wished I'd
done something, anything, for my baby, and now I had a chance to
purchase his burial plot. I felt like I was reclaiming my past, moving out
of the spot I'd been stuck in since the hour I learned my son had died.

Minutes later, the manager came back in the room and we sat
down again. He was a short man of Chinese descent, wearing a dark
blue suit, which seemed fitting for a cemetery office manager. He
spoke clearly; only the slightest hesitation and accent revealed that
English wasn't his first language.

As he took his place at the desk, he placed a large book before
him. He opened it to a page with many entries, and I realized that it
was used for record-keeping. Names and times were listed in it. Looking at the entry that the manager was pointing to, I saw my mother's
name under the heading, "Next of Kin." My baby was listed as Infant
Alleyne. There was a map of the area he was buried in and a note on
the measurements of the coffin.

I looked at the words "Infant Alleyne" and realized that if my mother had buried him with the name Godfrey, she would have been admitting that he was also Ralph's child. Smart move on her part.

"Is this your mother's signature?" the manager asked, pointing to the right hand corner.

"Yes."

"I've called our head office and explained what you've told me. Under normal circumstances, you wouldn't be able to buy the plot without written consent from the next of kin, which in this case is your mother. But if you can prove that you are the mother of the infant buried there, you may go ahead and buy it. Any hospital record or registration of the birth would be sufficient proof."

Things were looking up. I still had a few hours before the Registrar's office closed. I might be able to get the statement of birth or death, with my name on it, that very afternoon.

"Would it be possible for you to show me approximately where the grave is?" I asked. "I realize that we won't be able to find it with all the snow and ice, but I'd like to know the general area."

"That's no problem." The manager pulled his jacket from the rack behind the door, and followed me outside.

Freezing rain was now pouring down. Ignoring the weather, the manager took me over to section 11, and pointed straight ahead.

"It's just ahead. In the summertime, you can see that the infants' graves make a circle. When the weather is better you just need to look at the numbers."

"Thank you very much."

I returned to my car, started the engine and sat looking out through the rain to the area of the cemetery that held what I'd been looking for.

As I drove through the the cemetery gates, I realized that things were finally going to change. I could no longer resent my mother for keeping this address a secret. The important thing was what I did now that I knew.

I had one goal in visiting the Registrar's office: to get the documents I needed to make my case against my stepfather. As I started to fill out the request forms, I thought about how my grandmother always insisted that everything happened for a reason. If I could prevent this from happening to other people, like my nieces, maybe that would give a purpose to my pain.

Perhaps being raped and beaten, and then betrayed by my mother, was supposed to serve as a kind of life lesson. If that was the case, I supposed I deserved a passing grade for having survived thus far. Perhaps my lessons had prepared me to take my place in the fight against the sexual abuse of children. In that case, the finding of my son's grave would be my graduation, and now it was time to show the world that I was no longer just a victim of sexual abuse but a survivor.

I could hear my grandmother saying, "Is time to band yuh belly and come out fighting." The phrase meant that things were so out of control that you had nothing to lose, but you might have something to gain, even if it was only your pride. I remembered my grandfather explaining to me where "band yuh belly" came from.

"In de old days, we use to have stickfight. Was a big thing ... Yuh would get de best stick yuh could find and take cloth and tie yuh belly so yuh wouldn't get stick dey. Was a match jes like kung fu. De two opponents would come together and start fightin'. Yuh would try to hit yuh opponent before he could lash yuh. Yuh used to make sure yuh had yuh belly tie good because if yuh didn't yuh could get yuh belly puncture in de fight. No rules ... Jes fight like yuh mad and hope yuh around to brag bout it when it over. Of course, if yuh didn't take de time to band yuh head good, too, yuh wouldn't even be round for de rest a de fight. Yuh see, getting poke in yuh belly with a stick easier to deal with than getting hit in yuh head with it. That was how dey use to knock yuh out. Not like boxing when dey punch yuh out. Yuh opponent use to try and buss yuh head open. Yuh know how much time man come home with dey head buss open and bleeding."

I didn't really buy my grandfather's explanation. He sometimes added his own two cents' worth to his stories to make them more interesting. I didn't see why people would go out of their way to get hurt like that. But now I found myself thinking about the courage and strength these people must have possessed to take that risk.

I heard my number being called over the loudspeaker. It was my turn to see a clerk. I rose to my feet and took a seat at the counter where I saw a light flashing.

Five minutes later, the clerk handed me two legal-sized documents. I paid my fees and, holding the two documents in my hand, got up and headed downstairs. I didn't even look at them until I was seated comfortably in my car. Then I looked at the headings on the forms.

One was a "Statement of Live Birth" and the other a "Statement of Death." Not wanting to read any further just yet, I started my journey home.

I had succeeded more than I had anticipated, and now it took all my concentration to drive safely. When I entered my apartment, I decided to call Bev right away. It had been her idea to try the Registrar's office, so it seemed only fair that she should be the first person I told.

"So how do you feel?" Bev asked, sounding as excited as I was.

"I'm still shaking," I admitted. "What if this causes more problems?"

"I think you should give yourself time to be happy before you start worrying. You've waited long enough for this. Forget about what problems it might cause for anyone else. You're the one that matters, and you need to start thinking of you."

"It's so strange. I feel that now I'm allowed to cry when I want to, without feeling shame. I can feel the baby's presence more strongly now. It's like he's become real. Who would have thought that phoning the funeral homes would actually work? It seemed like such a long shot. Now your idea has worked too."

"Now you can take back some of the control you lost when it all happened," Bev told me. "You can see from the documents you have that it was all real. You have proof that your abuse and emotional pain were not just a nightmare. Your mind is allowing you to ask questions about what really happened, so you can search out the answers, start to heal yourself. One of the reasons you couldn't get on with your life is that there was so much deception. It's like you were brainwashed. When the people around you refused to discuss what happened and pretended that nothing had happened, you started to doubt yourself and your memories."

"That's exactly what happened," I agreed. "I've wondered whether I was crazy. Everyone involved went on with their life but me. My mother is still married to my stepfather, and they live like nothing important happened. My brothers have pushed the incidents out of their minds. Once when my stepfather raped me, my youngest brother stood near the door and watched. He was young, but he saw. Later, when I told my mother, he claimed he hadn't seen anything. I don't know whether my stepfather had convinced him that he really hadn't seen what he saw, or whether my mother scared him so much that he decided it just wasn't worth telling the truth."

"That's normal," Bev assured me. "They may have pushed the details out of their minds, the same way you did. Sometimes, it's easier to forget than to deal with confusing memories."

"My mother has been so deceitful. When she said that I was a troublemaker and a slut, sleeping with anyone and everyone, people just couldn't see any reason why a mother would say those things about her daughter if they weren't true. That's what the police thought when she gave her statement, when my stepfather was first arrested. When she took care of the funeral arrangements and was there in the hospital while I gave birth, she came across as the victim. It looked as if I'd gone out and done all this bad stuff and she'd stood by me. Like I was putting my mother through hell, and she was trying her best with a bad daughter."

"You have to allow yourself to feel the pain and the anger that you've been keeping inside for so long," Bev encouraged me. "You're right to question your mother's motives and actions. She owes you. You don't owe her."

"I still wonder whether I could have done something to help myself and stop Ralph."

"You were twelve years old," Bev reminded me. "There was only so much you could have done. Besides, you were new to the country and you had a lot of cultural differences to adjust to. You didn't rape your stepfather and get him pregnant. He did it to you. You are the victim. You can't blame yourself."

"I know. I just have to keep remembering that."

"Why don't you come to the office and see me tomorrow?"

Meet the person who had been my biggest help throughout the past few weeks? "I'll be there."

Later, I ran a hot bubble bath and poured myself some wine. I got into the tub and relaxed as the hot water covered my body. With my eyes closed and the lights dimmed, I felt good.

Something else was happening inside me. I was getting closer to making a connection with the little girl who was locked away in my past, the girl who I heard crying in my dreams. I couldn't hear her clearly when she spoke to me, but at least now I heard something. I'd felt her come alive when I was looking across the cemetery towards the grave. At that moment, I heard the crying stop and I could almost hear a lullaby being hummed. For the first time, I understood that she was waiting to be put to rest alongside her lost baby.

Enjoying the feel of the water against my skin, I let my mind stray. I concentrated on the blackness in my mind and tried to make contact. "Our search is almost over," I whispered. "I'm not going to let you down again ... You can come out if you want to ... You're a part of me, I know that now ... I'm not afraid of you ... I love you ... It's all right now ... "

CHAPTER TWENTY-SEVEN

The next day, I got a call from the Children's Aid Society. "I've contacted your three case workers, as you suggested," said the social worker. "They all remembered you when I described your case, and they've agreed to meet with you at our office in three weeks. Is that all right with you?"

"That's great!"

I was hoping that they would be able to fill in some of the blanks in my life. Looking over the notes I'd been taking for the past few months, I'd come to the conclusion that the Children's Aid Society had caused me a lot more problems than it had solved. I believed that when the CAS had taken me into care, its motives were good, but I felt cheated by its failure to care for me properly. My situation hadn't called for me to be tossed into homes with children who had broken the law. More appropriate shelters should be made available for children from abusive environments. Their cases are special.

On my way over to the Rape Crisis Centre, I made a list of the people who had let me down. First of all, the police department, for not doing a proper investigation. Testing could have been done to prove that the baby was indeed my stepfather's; then the police couldn't have concluded that there was a "lack of evidence". Secondly, the Children's Aid Society, which should have helped me get this case through court, instead of agreeing so readily with the Crown attorney. And thirdly, of course, there was my mother.

Upon my arrival at the Rape Crisis Centre, Bev, the counsellor who helped me believe that I could make a difference, offered me a hug. "It's good to finally meet you, Vanessa."

"It's really good to meet you."

I accepted a cup of coffee and followed Bev into her office. Following her lead, I lit a cigarette and made myself comfortable on a chair facing her. "I haven't looked these over yet," I admitted, handing her the documents I'd received from the Registrar's office. "I don't want to spoil this dream by finding that there's nothing here that I can use."

She looked the documents over silently for a minute or two. Then she said, "Do you realize that the names of the cemetery and the funeral home are listed on this statement of death?"

I got up, went over to her chair, and looked at the document. Written there was the information I had wanted for so long. I hadn't needed to call all those funeral homes.

"Why didn't I think of that before?" I sighed. "I should have gone to the Registrar's office right at the start."

"Well, stranger things have happened. I'm just happy that things are turning around for you."

"Do you think that I'm doing the right thing?"

"The only right thing is what is right for you, Vanessa. What makes you feel better in the long run is what is better for you," she answered. "You're not giving yourself enough credit. You've gone after what you wanted. It doesn't matter whether you decide to press charges against your stepfather or not. You've already won."

"It still doesn't seem fair that he got away with it."

"You're right. Although things have changed a lot, the system needs to change a lot more to allow victims their rights. Offenders do tend to get away with a lot. But it's stories like yours that will make people listen. When women see what you've been through, and the way you've handled it, they too will have the strength and courage to take charge of their own lives. You're a great example to all incest survivors and I'm proud of you."

I spent a bit more time with Bev. I could see the honesty in her face, and I hoped that someday I'd be able to feel as strongly about myself as she did.

The day finally came when I was to go to the Crown attorney's office on College Street to meet with one of their representatives. Earlier in the day, I met with a lawyer at the Barbara Schliffer Clinic. What she told me all but killed my hopes of charging my stepfather.

"Unfortunately, when a person has been tried once they cannot be tried again with the same crime."

I had heard that before. In fact, I'd heard it so many times over the past year that I was afraid I would soon start to believe it.

"You may be able to charge him with something other than what he was charged with then," the lawyer suggested. "I'll have to look at the circumstances of the withdrawal of the original charges."

"So you're saying that he is going to get away with what he did to me?"

"There are a few things I think you can do. I'll investigate the possibilities and get back to you. Things are changing, but very slowly."

I met Sergeant Wood at the Crown's office, and the Crown attorney arrived shortly afterwards. She showed us into the library, a room with shelves of large law books lining the walls and two tables in the centre. I sat down and took out all the material I had relating to my case.

After fifteen minutes of questions and answers, I had told her about my case and the better part of my life. She wanted the exact dates of the rapes, how they affected my life then and now, and my reasons for wanting to file new charges after all this time.

When she was satisfied with my side of the story, she turned to Sergeant Wood. He explained how he had investigated my case by interviewing my mother, my teacher, the Children's Aid Society and myself, and how this had led to my stepfather's arrest. He went over the details of my stepfather's release on bail, his preliminary hearing, and the Crown attorney's decision to drop the charges.

"I don't want to cause any trouble," I said. "I just want some answers and some justice. Half of me is trapped in the past, while the other half of me is trying to succeed at my career, and at being a good mother. Half the time I have no sense of belonging." I let my tears flow. "I remember things that make no sense to me. I share my life with a fourteen-year-old girl I can barely remember." I paused, trying to make sense of my crowded emotions. "Somewhere deep inside of me, I'm trapped at that point in my life. And you, I mean the justice system here in Canada, helped my stepfather hurt me. You told him it was all right. You let him go. My dreams are filled with his face, with his hands touching me. I don't even own my own mind."

"What do you want done?" the Crown asked.

"I want the Canadian justice system to apologize by picking up this case and finishing what it started," I said. "I want the police and the Crown's office to do whatever is necessary to help me press new charges. I want to make sure that my stepfather is prevented from messing up anyone else's life."

"All I can do is look into what you've shared with me. I'll be in touch with you," she promised. "It's not fair that you've had to go through so much."

On my way home, I thought about what I had accomplished. I had faced the officer who conducted the original investigation and I'd shown him what had happened to the fourteen-year-old he was suppose to Serve and Protect. Maybe in the future his investigations would be a bit more in-depth. Maybe the Crown attorney's office would be more careful in deciding which cases were worth pursuing.

CHAPTER
TWENTY-EIGHT

A week later, I was in Toronto again for the meeting with the three case workers at the Children's Aid Society's office. Being in that building brought back memories. It was there in the doctor's office that I was told that I was pregnant with my son, Josh. I remembered that day. I'd been feeling sick for a few weeks, and the doctor had suggested I take a pregnancy test. I had agreed, though I was sure the results would be negative. But when I went in that day, the nurse had told me, "It looks like you're going to have to deal with not feeling so well for a while, Vanessa. You're not sick, just pregnant."

I had barely been able to contain my joy. I hadn't thought about having children before, but after Christopher's death, I'd worried that I was going to be forced to remain childless.

Making my way up to the second floor, I thought about the many times I'd climbed these stairs before. Sometimes it was to meet with my workers, but most of the time it was to complain about the group homes and that I was being treated like a criminal.

I remembered one incident particularly. I'd gone to one of the sexual abuse group meetings the day before, and it had left me feeling very angry. I'd come to the Children's Aid Society to yell at my case worker for making me attend. The meeting had touched on something I didn't want to deal with — my mother's denial of the abuse.

With tears in my eyes, I'd walked up those very stairs and into my case worker Gwen's office.

"I have to speak to you," I'd demanded.

"I'm on the phone, Vanessa," Gwen had said. "Wait for a few minutes."

"I don't want to wait, I want to speak to you *now!*"

"I told you, I'm on the phone."

"I'm not leaving, so you may as well speak to me now."

She'd hung up. I could tell that she was angry. Of the three workers I had while in the care of the Children's Aid Society, I liked Gwen the best. She seemed sincerely concerned about my well-being. When I was rude to her, I always felt bad about it later on.

"Don't ever come in here and speak to me that way again," she'd scolded me. "I realize that you want to speak to me, but that does *not* give you the right to interrupt me while I'm on the phone. Now sit down and calm yourself."

"I don't want to go back to those stupid meetings. I always feel a lot worse afterwards. I want you to take me out."

"What happened?"

"I don't like talking about my personal problems with strangers, and I don't like hearing their personal problems."

It took her half an hour, but somehow Gwen had convinced me to try to at least get through the sessions, even if I didn't see any benefits right away.

Now, I had an appointment on the second floor.

"It's nice to finally meet you," said the social worker who had been doing the research for me. She showed me to a chair in the front corridor. The place had changed a lot. The offices had been shifted around, and where there had once been open offices, security doors were now in place.

A few minutes later, Elaine arrived. I recognized her and introduced myself.

"It's really good to see you, Vanessa," she said politely.

We sat down and talked about the changes in my life since the last time I'd seen her.

Gwen came in five minutes later. It occurred to me then that I always remembered her so clearly was because she'd spent the most time with me. Looking at her now, I realized that I was happy to see her. She didn't seem to have aged at all since 1985, when I'd last seen her.

Then Valerie arrived and the social worker who had arranged the meeting led us all into an empty room. Each case worker was given photocopies of the reports I had received from the Children's Aid Society, to refresh their memories of my case.

Knowing that the three women had no idea why I had asked to meet with them, I began to fill them in.

"First of all, I just want to thank each of you for taking the time to meet with me," I said. "I appreciate the opportunity to see you all again. I want you to know that it's all right if you're unable to answer some of my questions. The reason I'm here is that I've been trying to fill in the blanks in my memories of what happened to me while I was in the care of the Children's Aid Society." I looked at each of them as I spoke. They listened, nodding. "I'm really only trying to find myself," I went on. "I was hoping that you three could fill me in on what I was like back then. What was on my mind? Was I really as depressed as this report says I was? Anything that you could tell me about myself would really be of interest to me. I can't seem to connect with the girl that I was then. It's as if I was a different person. I want to know who I was, and what made me so unhappy."

They were all silent for a few minutes, scanning their copies of the reports I'd handed out. Gwen was the first to speak. "I don't know what to tell you, Vanessa. You were a lot more mature than any of my other cases at the time. I remember you clearly. You were organized, and I think that's the one thing that stood out the most. You were so *organized.*"

"I remember you being confused," said Valerie. "I was your first case worker, and I remember that you had a lot on your mind. I remember how upset you were about your mother denying your allegations. You felt rejected, and that caused you to cry a lot."

"I remember you the same way," agreed Elaine. "You were always preoccupied with what your mother was saying to the Children's Aid Society. You were always upset when you heard anything new."

"You hated talking about what happened between you and your stepfather," Gwen added. "If I remember correctly, you were very concerned about the baby you had, and you were searching for the reasons for his death, and trying to find his grave. At one point you asked me to find out about him from the hospital for you. Unfortunately, I didn't get the information until after you left our care."

"So I did talk about my baby?"

"You never brought up the subject outright. You hinted at it a lot. You have to realize that you didn't trust anyone, you always had your guard up."

"Did my mother ever try to get me back home with her?"

"No," said Valerie. "Right from the start, your mother claimed you were a liar. She said she'd brought you to Canada from Trinidad because no one there could control your behaviour. She never tried to contact you, though she was allowed access to you and could have visited you if she'd wanted. But she made it clear from the beginning that she supported your stepfather."

"From what I remember, you were never a problem to any of your workers," said Elaine. "You were so sad and confused about what was happening to you. You tried to get into trouble a few times in the group homes — destroying other residents' property, stealing things like kitchen knives and forks. I always wondered why you never stole anything you needed or could have used."

Gwen looked at me thoughtfully. "You know, Vanessa, one of the things that I remember most about you was the way you were always trying to make sense of things. It was as if you had all this information in your head, and you didn't know what to do with it. I remember feeling sorry for you. You seemed to be so overwhelmed. You wouldn't talk about what was bothering you, but you never stopped complaining about your group homes and the staff there. You were different. You shouldn't have been in a home with so many rules and restrictions. I remember how upset you were when your group home parents wouldn't let you stay up to write your poems. You stormed into my office the next day and insisted that you were never going back. I really regretted being unable to help you. While I was your worker, you ran away and were reported as AWOL dozens of time. Every time the police found you and brought you back, you were more unhappy."

We talked for over an hour. When the meeting was over, I thanked the women. We exchanged business cards, and I promised to let them know if I succeeded in filing charges against my stepfather. I was getting my things together to leave when Gwen stopped me.

"Do you think that the Children's Aid Society helped you at all?" she asked.

I sat down on the chair I had just vacated, and thought about the question. I'd never really thought about it before. "I guess the Children's Aid Society could take the credit for preventing me from being molested again. But, since the CAS was my legal guardian, I think the CAS should have taken the time to help investigate my allegations, or at least to help me find my baby's grave. Instead it just put me into one group home after another, with no consideration for my feelings. I had to follow the CAS's rules, live where it put me and then say thanks."

"Do you think that the Children's Aid Society should have been an advocate for your rights?" Gwen asked.

"Yes, I do," I answered without hesitation. "If the CAS wasn't going to help me, it should never have apprehended me in the first place. I will probably never have any sort of meaningful relationship with my brothers. None of us really got a proper chance to know each other. They all have children now, and I probably won't know them well either. Why? Because we all got caught up in a system that doesn't work. I can't change the past, and the past really sucks. The Children's Aid Society only made a bad situation worse."

CHAPTER
TWENTY-NINE

I drove straight from the Children's Aid Society to the cemetery, picking up some flowers on the way. At the front desk, I was greeted by the manager I'd met on my first visit. I gave him the documents I'd received from the Registrar's office and waited in his office while he made photocopies. He came back after a minute or two and handed me the Burial Rights Certificate and the receipts for the grave, which I'd just paid for.

"This is yours," he said. "What do you want on the memorial?"

"Can I put whatever I want on it?"

"Anything you like."

I started working on the design. ALLEYNE would appear in big letters at the very top. Under that it would say, *In loving memory of my dear son, Christopher.*

Finally, I had kept my promise to him. I'd bought his grave, and now he was going to have a memorial. He'd never be forgotten now. I wanted to stand on his grave. I wanted to feel his presence and let him know that I was there, that I had found him, that I wasn't going to let him go.

Once I'd completed all the paperwork, the manager led me out to the grave. He showed me the numbers that marked the spot where Christopher lay, then he went back inside. It had started to rain while I was inside; patches of snow still lay on the ground.

I felt my energy drain away as I stood before the grave. Weeping quietly, I thanked God for taking me there. My head felt empty. My knees started to shake, and I couldn't keep them from buckling. On my knees in the mud, I traced the numbers on my son's grave with my fingertips. I could feel my anger and pain start to melt into a strange peace as I greeted my son. I found myself lying face down in the cold, muddy snow and ice. I lay on my baby's grave and cried.

I could feel the lost girl coming out to be with her child. As I cried for my son, she cried for her freedom. I heard the groaning and moaning that I'd heard so many times in my nightmares. She shook within my body. For a moment, we were one, then I felt her working loose, bit by bit. She let me love her and make peace with her. And then I felt her begging me to let her go. I did. I set her free. Free to rest and die … to be with the child she had been yearning for all these years …

Just when I thought she was totally gone, she nudged me and thanked me for listening — for helping her find her way.

When I got up from the grave and started towards my car, I felt free and happy. My coat was drenched in mud, my hands were dirty, my legs were still shaking and I still had tears in my eyes. But I felt lighter. I was no longer carrying the burdens of a mourning fourteen-year-old mother. She remained at the grave with her child.

Now I could go on with my life and do what I had to do, including filing charges against my stepfather, and working to prevent this from happening again. I wasn't angry any more. I wasn't desperate to get things done right away. Even if it took the rest of my life, I would bring sexual abuse out into the open. I had all the time in the world.

One thing was clear in my mind: This was the end of a chapter, not the end of the whole book.

CHAPTER THIRTY

A few weeks after I met with the Crown attorney, a police detective contacted me. The Crown had reviewed my case and was willing to try it in court. I almost jumped out of my skin with joy when I heard the news. A month later, I was sitting in the police station, and two officers were taking my statement.

My stepfather was arrested again, and again my mother posted his bail. But this time around, I was being kept informed.

In 1992 and 1993, my stepfather spent a lot of time appearing in court and having his case remanded. Once the judge at the pre-trial hearing decided that there was enough evidence for my case to proceed to trial, I had nothing much to do but wait and see. September 27, 1993, was the date set for the trial to begin, but my stepfather had problems with his lawyer and the trial was postponed until March 28, 1994.

I knew that anything could happen. The court might decide not to put my stepfather through a new trial, since the charges were dropped back in 1983. Or the court might try him and decide that he was not guilty, and he might leave the courthouse a free man. But whatever happened, I knew I was now strong enough to handle it. And I was positive that Ralph Godfrey would never really be a free man — not until he could ask for and receive my forgiveness.

CHAPTER THIRTY-ONE

y old friend Ted came through for me after all. A few months after I called him, he gave me the addresses and telephone numbers of Paul and Peter Turnbull. I went down to New York City to visit them for a few days. I was hoping they'd be able to tell me who my father was.

I kept my tape recorder running while they reminisced about my mother and my aunt Daisy. I enjoyed the sound of their voices. They no longer had Trinidadian accents, but now had the sound of Brooklyn and even some Jamaican patois mixed into their speech. Judging from the friends they kept, I suspected they'd led quite eventful lives since my birth in 1968.

I also contacted Daisy, who now lived in another state. I asked her if she knew whether Paul might be my father. At first she denied even knowing the twins, but when I asked her about her engagement to Peter back in the late sixties, she suddenly remembered. She agreed that the possibility did exist.

Paul's family tried hard to convince me that Paul was my father, but I found that I didn't really care any more. I had survived for so long without a father; maybe having one wasn't so important after all. Besides. Paul's family had their own problems, which made me think twice about getting involved. God knows I had enough headaches trying to sort things out with the Alleynes.

The only time I mentioned the brothers' names to my mother was just before Christmas 1993. I wanted to give her a chance to tell me herself whether Paul was my father, so I phoned her and asked her straight out. She was neither hostile nor particularly friendly, but she did speak to me. She denied that Paul was my father, and she refused to tell me who my father was. She wouldn't answer yes or no when I asked her whether she had been raped.

When I told her that I had to take my stepfather to court for my own sake, her response surprised me: "I don't believe in dragging up the past, Pet. But if that's what you have to do, then go ahead and do it."

I guess wonders never cease, I thought. Maybe my mother and I had a chance at real togetherness after all.

EPILOGUE

By the end of April, 1994, the trial was over.

The final round of questioning had been rough for me. By the last morning of my testimony, I'd known it wasn't going to be easy to prove my claims. My friend Trish was the only witness on my behalf, and most of what she'd had to say had been considered hearsay. My stepfather had had a lot more support than I did. My mother and my brothers were going to testify on his behalf, and as I walked out of the courtroom I saw my mother's friend Paula sitting next to her. That was hard for me to take. Over the years, Paula had always claimed to be on my side. I wasn't really surprised, but I'd been holding on to hope, and having to face the truth was painful for me.

I didn't stay to hear my brothers testify that day. I left the court-house and went to the Rape Crisis Centre with Bev. Throughout the trial, through the long nights when I'd thought I just couldn't go on anymore, Bev had been my strength. She'd always reminded me that we'd come a lot further that either of us had thought possible.

We sat in her office and quietly went over the past two years. The quest for justice had been long and frustrating.

"You understand, Vanessa, that the Crown made an agreement with your stepfather's lawyer that things would be weighted in your stepfather's favour if you couldn't give the exact dates of the rapes. Even if the jury decides you're telling the truth, the judge will have to stand by that agreement."

I sighed. "It's been over ten years. I remember the approximate times that he raped me, but I can't remember the exact dates. And I wasn't going to lie and make them up. If the Crown really wanted to prove my case, all it had to do was run a DNA test on the baby's blood and compare it to my stepfather's DNA. The hospital confirmed that it still has samples of Christopher's blood on file — more than enough to do a test on. But now we're right back where we started."

"No matter what happens, remember, you did your part. Your mother, your brothers, and their friends will have to live with their testimony — and pray to God that none of the younger children pay the price."

The telephone rang. It was the detective in charge of the case, calling to tell Bev that my mother had started her testimony.

With my mother's support, and my brothers' claim that Ralph was a good father, Ralph himself never even had to take the stand. I knew that my battle to get justice through the legal system was over. I had lost. A few days later, Bev called me and confirmed that Ralph had been acquitted.

"Remember, Vanessa, we never expected to get this far. You had only yourself on your side. Your stepfather had everyone else. And you have accomplished something important: if any of your nieces ever find themselves in your position, they'll be able to use your testimony."

I wasn't surprised, but that didn't ease my disappointment.

My phone kept ringing. Many of the women who had supported me throughout the trial called to offer sympathy. The detective in charge of the case called to confirm the verdict.

"Even if he hadn't gotten off with your mother's testimony," he explained, "he would most likely have walked on the double jeopardy issue. His lawyers would have played those cards in an appeal — a guilty verdict would have been overturned eventually. But right from the start you've maintained that a guilty verdict isn't what you really wanted, that you were doing this because you wanted to prevent your stepfather from doing to anyone else what he did to you. If you ask me, I think you've succeeded. If nothing else, you forced him and your mother to think about what they did to you. I doubt they'll make the same mistake again, now that they've seen what can happen."

I was grateful for the support that was coming my way. I think people were surprised by my silence about the verdict. Maybe that's why they felt compelled to try to explain to me the workings of the justice system. But the acquittal wasn't what had me speechless. I had known going in that our chances of winning the case were next to nothing; that is the experience of many abuse victims. What shocked me into silence was my mother's continuing support of my stepfather. She'd had all those years to think about what he'd done and about how she'd let him do it. Now she had shown the court, my family and me that he would always come first. She had broken the link between us, and I knew that no matter how much I wanted to hold on to the hope that maybe one day she would love me, I had to let go. My mother is now dead to me and to my children.

There was one more thing I had to do.

I placed the flowers on my son's grave and knelt beside it one last time. I closed my eyes and felt the tension and pain seeping out of my body along with my tears. I wept for the mother and family I never really had and for the son I never even got to hold. I wept and said goodbye.

Back in my own home that night, I thought about my stepfather, my mother, and their friends and family. They'd be outside in her backyard, having a barbecue and celebrating their victory. They were going on with their lives. Well, so was I. And I too had something to celebrate. I had accomplished what I set out to do: I'd forced my parents to face what they had done. I'd found out where my baby was buried. I was now free to move out of the past, leave the nightmares and the hurt. I had a new lease on life, and I intended to make the best of it.

I poured myself a sherry, lit a cigarette, curled up on my living room sofa and turned my thoughts toward my future.

Publisher's Acknowledgements

A special thanks to Nadia Halim and Patricia K. Murphy for their critical, sensitive and supportive editing; and to Ramabai Espinet for her creole editing skills.